Marguerite Patten's
MULTI-MIXER COOKBOOK

Marguerite Patten's
MULTI-MIXER COOKBOOK

Collins Glasgow and London

Metrication

Both metric and imperial measures are given in this book, for in the future we shall be buying some foods that are labelled with only metric weights and measures. These are very easy to follow, in fact if you have children at school they will be fully conversant with them, for these measures have been taught for several years now. Information on metrication is given below.

One golden rule is to follow *either* the metric measures *or* the imperial ones, for that way you keep everything in proportion. *Do not* 'dodge' from column to column. If you and your children use this book, you may prefer to use imperial measures and they the metric measures learned at school.

Weights

We will weigh in grams (g) instead of ounces (oz), and kilograms (kg) not pounds (lb). The accurate conversion is:

28·35 g equals 1 oz

1 kg equals 2·2 lb

It has been decided to take 25 g as 1 oz; when you get to larger quantities, i.e. above 6 oz, you need to step up the amount of grams to give similar quantities of food, *e.g.*

6 x 25 equals 150 g, which is appreciably less than 6 oz, so I call 6 oz – 175 g which gives the same quantity as 6 oz. In most cases in this book 4 oz is given as 100 g, but in a pudding or cake, when I want the measurements to be exact, I remind you to be a little more generous with flour, etc., by weighing 110 g or a generous 100 g. Sometimes 0·5 kg is shown as 1 lb; this is when you need not be bothered about slight differences between metric and imperial. Where I think it is important to be accurate I call 1 lb – 450 g.

Liquids

The measure here is a litre; 1 litre equals 1·75 pints (pt). Where small quantities are required, we use millilitres (ml) in this book; elsewhere you may see decilitres (dl). 142 ml (or 1·5 dl) is the equivalent of $\frac{1}{4}$ pint. Although often 125 ml is given as the equivalent of $\frac{1}{4}$ pint, I feel that is a little low for cooking, so I give 150 ml. Where the quantity of liquid does not need to be too exact 1 pint is expressed as a generous 0·5 litre.

Acknowledgments

Cover photograph by David Levin

Photographs by permission of: British Duck Advisory Bureau page 69; Danish Food Centre, London page 80; General Foods Kitchens, Mellow Birds Instant Coffee (Lexington) page 72; Lea and Perrins page 37; New Zealand Lamb page 65; Olives from Spain page 33; White Fish Kitchen and Potato Marketing Board pages 41, 45.

First published 1981
Published by William Collins Sons and Company Limited
© Marguerite Patten 1981
Composition in Rockwell by Filmtype Services Limited, Scarborough, North Yorkshire
Printed in Great Britain

ISBN 411212 1

CONTENTS

INTRODUCTION

For many years now a mixer has been an accepted appliance in many kitchens. We have become used to putting ingredients into a mixer, instead of arduously beating, stirring or whisking by hand.

The development of blenders or liquidizers (whichever name you prefer) also meant that many troublesome and time-consuming preparations and processes were quickly, easily and efficiently accomplished.

One might have thought that this was the end of the inventiveness of designers, but year by year separate attachments to use with some mixers began to emerge, and cooks found these of value for specific purposes such as grating, shredding, juice extracting, mincing, etc.

One of the latest aids in preparing ingredients for a wide range of sweet and savoury recipes is a food processor.

I am often asked by people 'Should I have a mixer or should I have a processor?' I think it is important to realize that they are not identical. The processor will do some of the jobs a mixer will do, not all, but a mixer is not as versatile as a food processor. I describe exactly what the various appliances will do in the first chapter. If you own these pieces of equipment it may help you to decide just which to select for a given job. If you are thinking about buying a type of mixer I hope this chapter will act as a short guide as to what you may expect from each piece of equipment.

The recipes in this book have been selected to demonstrate the great scope of these appliances. For example, I think many busy people often avoid making puréed soups since it means washing up a sieve after use. Nowadays a blender or food processor will produce a beautifully smooth soup from meat, vegetables or poultry. The 'hard work' of making a cake lies in the initial beating, creaming or whisking. If you leave the mixer to do these tasks you then have time to prepare the cake tins, weigh the flour, etc. so the whole operation is done quickly and with little effort. I discuss quite fully just where the mixer is so good in preparing cakes and where, in my opinion, one should take over and mix in the flour by hand. You will also find my personal recommendations for using a food processor for mixing cakes, etc.

Readers will appreciate that each make of mixer, blender or food processor will have certain individual features, but the basic principle behind their design is the same. That is why this book will be of value whichever model you may possess.

Today you can, of course, purchase very sophisticated equipment, including a blender which will also cook the food after preparation, but that does not affect how you make the initial dish.

I hope you enjoy using this book, and that it will increase your knowledge and pleasure in using your particular mixer, blender or food processor.

Marguerite Patten

CHAPTER 1

RANGE OF MIXERS

Many readers may have some or all of the mixer equipment, i.e. a mixer with some attachments, a blender and/or a food processor. This means they have a wide choice when preparing a dish. To help you make the wisest selection, you will see that recipes give the recommended equipment before listing the ingredients.

Here is a brief summary of which equipment is best for basic preparations.

Selecting the equipment

The following advice is based upon tests over a prolonged period.

PÂTÉS (see pages 20 to 23)
1st choice   Food processor. This deals with larger amounts than a blender.
2nd choice   Blender.
3rd choice   Mincer attachment. Useful for mincing ingredients, but does not blend.

SOUPS (see pages 25 to 42)
1st choice   Blender. You can add all the liquid as well as the solid ingredients.
2nd choice   Food processor. Best results if the solid ingredients are puréed first, then liquid added later.

FISH (see pages 43 to 48)
1st choice   Food processor. This can chop raw fish as evenly as needed.
2nd choice   Mincer attachment. Slower.
3rd choice   Blender. Can chop small amounts of shellfish, less good for white fish.

MEAT AND POULTRY (see pages 49 to 63)
1st choice   Food processor. Chops raw or cooked meat, boned poultry and game perfectly and with great speed.
2nd choice   Mincer attachment. Slower.
3rd choice   Blender. Deals with small amounts of tender cooked meat.

SAUCES (see pages 68 to 76)
1st choice   Blender or Food Processor.

STUFFINGS (see pages 76 to 78)
1st choice   Food processor. Deals with larger amounts than a blender.
2nd choice   Blender.
3rd choice   Mincer or mixer attachments. Restricted value.

VEGETABLES (see pages 79 to 81)
1st choice   Food processor. Chops or slices quickly.
2nd choice   Mixer attachments. Slightly less speedy.
3rd choice   Blender. Restricted value.

PASTRY (see page 84)
1st choice   Food processor. If great care taken not to over-handle the dough.
2nd choice   Mixer.

CAKES (see pages 85 to 90)
1st choice   Mixer attachment. This aerates the mixture better than a food processor. Some cakes are impossible to make in a food processor, i.e. whisked sponges.
2nd choice   Food processor. Quite satisfactory for many mixtures.

BREAD (see pages 91 to 92)
1st choice   Mixer with dough hook.
2nd choice   Food processor. Use with care, so the dough is not over-handled.

Symbols used in this book

Each recipe shows the appliance or appliances suitable for preparing the dish.

Ⓑ   Blender (also known as a liquidizer) explained on page 10.
ⒻⓅ   Food processor, explained on page 12.
Ⓜ   Mixer, explained on page 8.
ⓂⒶ   Mixer Attachments (detailed in the recipe) explained on pages 14, 15 and 16.

A mixer

The term 'electric mixer' is used to describe a wide range of mixing appliances. There are small *portable mixers* (*Fig 1*) which simply have two whisks (often called 'beaters'). These mixers are used with your own basins or mixing bowls, as they have no stand or special mixing bowl.

There are small to *medium-sized mixers* which can be used on a stand with the mixing bowl supplied (*Fig 2*) but often the motor and beaters can be detached from the stand and the appliance used as a portable mixer. These smaller mixers usually have a choice of two speeds.

Lastly there is the table type mixer, i.e. a *large mixer on a stand* with its own mixing bowl (*Fig 3*). This type of mixer is supplied with a whisk, to deal with lighter mixtures, and a heavier beater. The latter is used for rubbing fat into flour, creaming and beating actions. (Many other attachments, described and illustrated on pages 14–16 can be obtained. These include a dough hook, used for kneading yeast mixtures.)

What will an electric mixer do?

The processes given below apply to the basic mixer. Obviously you extend the value of a mixer if you purchase the optional attachments.

A mixer will:
1 **Beat** together the ingredients for icings, see page 91, and complete cake and pudding mixtures made by the melting method. A low speed is advisable at the beginning of the process, but often this is increased.

2 **Cream** fat and sugar for cakes, puddings, fillings for cakes, and also mash and cream vegetables. It is important to have the ingredients at room temperature. The process of creaming can be hastened and made more efficient if the mixing bowl and whisk or beater are warmed, by filling the bowl with hot water and standing the whisk or beater in this for a few minutes. Dry the bowl and attachment well before using. Do not melt the fat unless the recipe tells you to.

Choose a low speed for this process, see page 86. You may need to scrape the sides of the bowl once or twice to make sure that all the mixture is being beaten evenly. Eggs should be added

Fig 1 A small portable electric mixer.

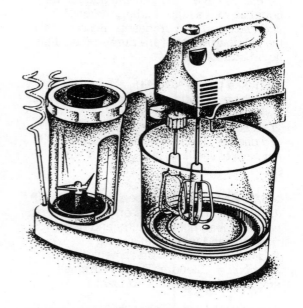

Fig 2 A medium-sized mixer that can be used on a stand, or lifted off and treated as a portable mixer.

slowly. Flour can be added in some recipes with the machine in operation, see page 86.

Keep the whisks of a *portable mixer* moving around in the bowl so that all the fat and sugar are evenly creamed.

If using a *mixer on a stand*, check that the beater is reaching the ingredients at the bottom of the bowl. If any fat and sugar are left unmixed the beater needs lowering; follow the manufacturer's instructions for doing this.

3   **Emulsify** eggs and oil in mayonnaise, although a blender or food processor will do this more rapidly and with less effort.

4   **Knead** biscuit and yeast doughs. A special dough hook gives the best result for yeast mixtures.

5   **Mash** potatoes and other vegetables, see page 81.

6   **Rub fat into flour.** The fat can be taken from the refrigerator. It should be cut into small pieces and dropped into the flour, or flour and salt or sugar. Switch on to the lowest speed. Watch this process carefully, for over-mixing will give a dough that is difficult to handle.

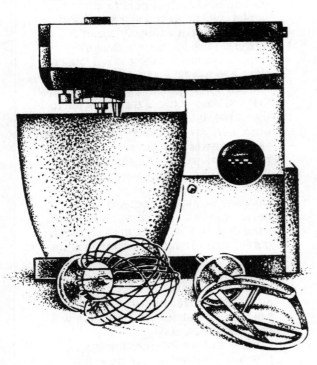

Fig 3 A large mixer that has to be on the stand with the bowl supplied by the manufacturer.

The process takes only about 30 seconds and you should switch off as soon as the mixture looks like fine breadcrumbs. The liquid can be added slowly and gradually with the machine operating at low speed.

7   **Whisk** egg whites, cream and other light ingredients.

Higher speeds are generally recommended, but see the specific instructions under the various recipes.

To use a mixer correctly

a) Read the manufacturer's instructions carefully regarding the maximum quantities with which the mixer will deal. If you exceed these you will be dissatisfied with the results obtained.

b) Appreciate the techniques required for the various processes. For example, when kneading a mixture by hand you do this slowly and deliberately; if using the mixer, adjust the speed to give the slowest movement possible.

Egg whites are whisked very briskly by hand, therefore you should use the maximum speed possible when whisking these with an electric mixer.

c) Do not over-mix. Many disappointing results are caused by allowing the mixer to beat, cream or whisk for too long.

d) Never try and scrape the mixture in the bowl with a spatula or knife *while* the machine is in operation, you could damage the beater. Switch off, then scrape down the mixture from the sides of the bowl.

e) Use a rubber spatula to remove the mixture from the bowl; these are excellent for scraping out the last of the food, and do not harm the bowl.

Caring for a mixer

Keep the motor of a mixer clean by wiping it with a damp cloth; never immerse this part in water.

Remove the beater from the mixer and wash thoroughly, taking great care that the wire whisk is not bent or distorted.

The mixing bowl belonging to the mixer can be washed in a very hot detergent solution; dry it well. Never put plastic bowls into a heated oven.

Store the mixer and attachments carefully. A mixer, or similar appliance, is of greatest value if it stands on a working surface so that it is easily available for use.

Wall brackets are available for some portable mixers.

A blender

Blenders, which are also referred to as 'liquidizers', have been on the market now for many years. You can obtain a blender as a separate appliance with its own electric motor or as an accessory to an electric mixer. Blenders are available in various sizes, but the goblet is always shaped rather like a flower vase with a lid. Original blenders were made of glass but many modern ones are now produced from a durable plastic (*Fig 4*). I have used the term 'blender' (rather than liquidizer) in this book, as it is the one more often selected by manufacturers.

How does a blender work?

At the bottom of the goblet (the name given to the container as opposed to the complete blender machine, and used throughout this book) you will find there are several blades. When the motor is switched on, these blades revolve at a great speed, so achieving results very quickly.

Fig 4 A typical blender (often called a liquidizer).

What will a blender do?

1 **Chop and grind** dry ingredients, such as raw or cooked vegetables, breadcrumbs, nuts, well-dried herbs, firm cheese, ingredients for stuffings, etc. It is *inadvisable*, though, to use the blender for grinding coffee beans unless the manufacturer of your particular blender has stated it is suitable. You can buy separate electric coffee grinders or attachments for some mixers.

   One of the emergency measures for which you can use a blender is for grinding granulated sugar finely to take the place of caster sugar. If ground even more finely it becomes icing sugar. You may find it does not have quite such a perfect white colour as the ready-prepared icing sugar.

   You can grind nuts, such as blanched almonds, until they have the fineness of commercially prepared ground almonds.

   Certain vegetables can be finely chopped, so can orange or lemon rind. You will find information about preparing vegetables in the Soup and Vegetable chapters, pages 26 and 79.

2 **Takes the place of a sieve** Put cooked or raw fruit and vegetables, portions of cooked meat, fish or poultry in the goblet, switch on and in a very short time you have a relatively smooth mixture. I use the term 'relatively smooth' because in the case of tomato skins and seeds, raspberry pips or cooked celery pieces you may well find that you have some of these still left in the purée. If the recipe requires an absolutely smooth purée, then you must sieve afterwards to get rid of the small particles of skin, seeds etc. Sieving after liquidizing becomes a very simple task.

3 **Emulsify** various ingredients. This means you can blend several kinds of food, or liquid, together in the blender goblet, and produce a smooth mixture, i.e. blending oil and eggs to produce mayonnaise; recipes are on page 71.

   You can use the blender to produce an absolutely smooth texture in many sauces, more about this technique will be found on page 68.

   Pâtés and similar mixtures can be prepared in minutes, see page 20.

   Mothers of small children will find the blender a great asset in producing baby foods; suggested ideas are on page 93.

The speed with which ingredients are emulsified together in a blender means there is less possibility of curdling. You can therefore incorporate acid fruits into milk, custards, etc. as in Fruit Foule, recipes for which are on page 82 or Fresh Fruit Milk Shakes, page 18.

4 **Mix** drinks of all kinds, ranging from milk shakes to sophisticated beverages. You will find information about these on pages 17 to 18.

It is **essential** to crush ice, for cold drinks, **before** it is placed into the blender goblet; large cubes of ice can harm the blades.

To use a blender correctly

If the goblet is made of glass you must, of course, treat this very carefully. Warm the goblet before adding hot liquids or food.

Filling the goblet

a) There are many reminders throughout the book about the best way to fill the blender goblet. Some mixtures rise quite drastically in the goblet when it is switched on; it is therefore important that the goblet is never over-filled, otherwise the contents could force off the lid.

b) When using the blender you may find that, after a few seconds, the blades at the base of the goblet cease to turn. This is an indication that you have placed too much food into the goblet and this is constricting the blades. All you need to do is to switch off, remove some of the mixture, then switch on again. Often you will find that the goblet **will** take larger quantities if you feed the food through the removed centre cap in the lid, see Covering the Goblet. However, it is better to work with small batches of a mixture rather than try to fill the goblet.

c) Check that no tiny bones or fruit stones are placed into the blender goblet. If, by any chance, these were not observed when filling the container you will hear a high-pitched tone as the blades encounter the hard object. Switch off **immediately**, remove the mixture, check to see what is causing the problem. Never try to prod the blades or the mixture, with a sharp knife. This could catch the blades and cause them to become misshapen. Do not touch the blades with your fingers. A plastic spatula is the ideal utensil to scrape food out of the goblet.

Covering the goblet

Check that the lid is firmly in position before switching on.

If the recipe recommends adding food gradually, remove the centre cap from the lid. If your model does not have this cap, use a foil cover and cut out a centre hole (*Fig 5a*). You could also make a large funnel to fit snugly in the top of the goblet (*Fig 5b*).

Fig 5a If your blender does not possess a lid with a removable centre cap, cover the goblet with a foil lid – with a hole removed.

Fig 5b You may find it easier to feed food into the goblet if you fit a firm foil funnel into the centre hole in the lid.

Never remove the lid when the machine is in operation.

Speed to select

In most cases it is better to switch gradually from the lowest speed to that recommended in the recipe. By doing this you reduce the initial impetus that might force off the lid.

The choice of speed is important for the best results.

Caring for a blender

Never put the motor of a blender into water, keep clean by wiping with a damp cloth. A blender goblet and lid must be kept scrupulously clean. They come into contact with various kinds of foods and liquids and should be cleaned well every time after use. Wash and rinse well. Some blenders have a base that is easily removed when cleaning the goblet.

If the foods that have been blended are sticky, you may find it rather difficult to clean the goblet. In this case, half-fill the goblet with warm water, add one or two drops of liquid detergent, put on the lid and switch on for just a few seconds. After using detergent you should then rinse the goblet several times with clean water.

Do not put the lid on immediately after the goblet has been washed. Dry with a clean teacloth, being careful to avoid touching the sharp blades with your fingers, then allow it to stand uncovered at room temperature for a while. In this way you avoid the smell of tightly sealed damp equipment.

If using a blender that can be taken apart for cleaning, put together carefully, for example do make certain that the rubber ring at the base of the goblet is correctly replaced; also that the goblet is firmly and correctly seated on its base. If this is not done you may well find liquids leaking from the base. Obviously, all rubber rings must be replaced with new ones when they become too thin to be effective or have perished. It is therefore a wise precaution to have a new rubber ring in reserve. Remember that rubber, or synthetic rubber, should not be dried near dry heat.

A food processor

Food processors are relatively new domestic appliances but they are gaining rapidly in popularity. A food processor consists of a bowl-shaped container with a lid, which is placed on an electric motor. The bowl is made of a very durable plastic (*Fig 6*).

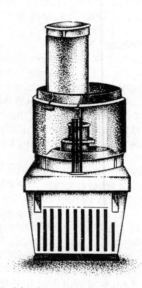

Fig 6 A typical food processor.

Fig 7 The metal knife supplied with food processors. This has various names, i.e. cutting, chopping or double-bladed knife.

How does a food processor work?

The most usual and useful cutting device in a food processor is the double-bladed steel cutting knife (*Fig 7*). When the lid is fixed in position and the motor switched on, this knife revolves at great speed, cutting and chopping food or emulsifying ingredients. There are other attachments which can take the place of this double-bladed knife, the main ones being a shredding (or grating) disc and a slicing disc.

Some machines also include discs that shred cabbage for coleslaw and prepare potatoes for chips; attachments to extract the juice from citrus fruits, and also a more complex attachment to extract the juice from other fruits and vegetables.

A plastic mixing knife is often supplied; this blends soft mixtures.

Food processors, unlike blenders and mixers, rarely have speed control. Often the contact between the lid and the bowl switches the machine on or off. A later development on some food processors is a switch, known as a pulse, which enables you to stop and start the machine without touching the lid, or the switch by the main electric socket.

Food processors carry out the various processes at great speed and it is very important to become accustomed to this so that you can gauge correctly the time required.

What will a food processor do?

A food processor carries out most of the functions of a blender, but has the advantage of being able to deal with rather larger amounts of certain mixtures. This is particularly useful when preparing pâtés, stuffings, etc. It can take the place of an electric mixer when preparing some cakes, shortcrust pastry, etc.; blending and kneading yeast mixtures, see pages 86, 84 and 92, and point 5 on page 92.

Most food processors will chop raw or cooked meat, fish or poultry more easily and as finely as the mincer attachment of a mixer; this is achieved within a matter of seconds. A food processor is not as efficient as a blender for making drinks, and its speed is too great to prepare the whisked type of sponge or to make a meringue mixture, although some processors do have the capability of whisking egg whites.

The food processor will

1 **Chop and grind** dry ingredients such as raw or cooked vegetables, breadcrumbs, nuts, well-dried herbs, firm cheese, etc.; either use the double-bladed cutting knife or the disc recommended by the manufacturer. When making stuffings you can first chop the breadcrumbs, herbs, onion, etc., then drop in the fat and egg and allow the food processor to bind the stuffing ingredients together.

2 **Sieve**, as described under Blenders, page 10. The food processor is *less* effective than a blender if a large amount of liquid is tipped into the bowl *with* the solid ingredients, e.g. when puréeing the ingredients for a soup, see page 25. On the other hand, the very sharp knife often chops tomato skins and rather stringy pieces of celery so efficiently that sieving is not required.

3 **Emulsify** mixtures most efficiently, including oil and eggs for mayonnaise, see page 71. The double-bladed cutting knife is used for this purpose. Pâtés of all kinds can be prepared, and the food processor is ideal for preparing baby's meals.

4 **Blend** the ingredients for many types of cakes, pastry, breads, icings, fillings and ice creams. Liquids can be added through the feed-tube to bind the various ingredients together. Vegetables may be beaten to a smooth cream.

5 **Slice and chop** vegetables, cheese etc. The slicing and chopping (grating) discs which are used make the preparation of sliced or uniformly chopped vegetables and cheese very simple. The secret is to push the ingredients through the feed-tube with the plastic pusher. Do not use your fingers or add too great a quantity of food at one time. The thickness of the slices can be determined to a degree – the harder you press on the pusher, the thicker the slices will be.

To use a food processor correctly

a) Read the manufacturer's recommendations carefully and appreciate fully how you lock the lid in position, particularly if this starts the machine.

b) Never try and remove the lid when the machine is operating, always wait until the motor has stopped.
c) Do not over-fill the bowl of the food processor; with most machines you will find you are advised that liquid should be no higher than the centre spindle.

   Most food processors have a circuit-breaker. If the machine is overloaded or used for too long a period the motor may overheat, and as a safeguard the motor will automatically cut out. After a period of up to about 30 minutes the machine will operate once again.
d) Food processor bowls are made to withstand very hot ingredients, but never put the bowl into a heated oven.
e) To avoid liquids splashing, add through the feed-tube with the machine in operation.
f) The cutting knife has extremely sharp blades; handle and wash this with the utmost care and keep in a safe place when not in use.

Caring for a food processor
The base of the food processor, which contains the electric motor, must not be immersed in water. Simply wipe with a damp cloth.

Keep the bowl, lid (including the feed-tube), the plastic pusher and the cutting device scrupulously clean. All of these can be immersed in a detergent solution. They should be rinsed well after washing.

Dry the parts of the food processor thoroughly after cleaning.

Do not store the food processor with the bowl and lid locked in position over the motor, simply place the lid on the bowl. Leave the plastic pusher out of the feed-tube to allow the air to circulate in the bowl.

Extra attachments

Most manufacturers offer attachments, many at additional cost to the basic machine. The following are examples of those available for food processors or mixers. Before ordering extra attachments consider their value, and whether they will duplicate others. For example, if you have a food processor with slicing and chopping discs you will not require these attachments for a mixer. A food processor can also take the place of a mincer.

Attachments for the food processor
All processors are supplied with a double-bladed knife, the name of which varies from 'chopping', 'cutting' or 'metal' knife.

Food processors also have both a slicing and shredding (grating) disc; some manufacturers provide more than two. These are described on page 13.

The additional items you may find included with your processor, or can purchase as optional extras are
1 **PLASTIC, DOUBLE-BLADED KNIFE** used for gentle processes such as blending mayonnaise or ice cream.
2 **SHORT DOUGH BLADE** has been introduced.
3 **WIDER CUTTING PLATES** for thicker slices of cabbage, etc.
4 **POTATO CHIP SLICER**, see page 66.
5 **JUICE EXTRACTOR** similar to that described on page 16.
6 **JUICE SEPARATOR**, again similar to that described on page 16.

Attachments for the mixer
The most usual attachments are described on the pages that follow. There are so many that I have put first those I consider of greatest value.

1 **CREAM MAKER** With the cost of dairy cream rising you may like to prepare cream from unsalted butter and milk. The recipes on page 75 show how to make a pouring (single) and thick

(double) cream. The cream can be used in all recipes but is particularly suitable for ice cream and jellied desserts.

Use the cream maker on a slow to medium speed. Dismantle after use, wash in hot detergent solution, rinse well in clear water and dry. Leave all parts at room temperature, but away from direct heat, for a while to make quite sure they are absolutely dry before reassembling.

2 **DOUGH HOOK** This attachment is fitted in place of the beater or whisk (*Fig 8*). The function of the dough hook is to mix and knead yeast mixtures. The hook pulls and stretches the dough, so imitating the movements of hand kneading.

Use a low speed with this attachment. Wash and dry the dough hook after use.

Fig 8 A typical dough hook.

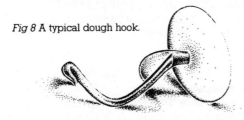

3 **MINCER** This fits into the mixer; follow the specific instructions given by the manufacturer for assembling the various parts.

Most mincer attachments can deal with raw and cooked meat, poultry, game and fish. It is also possible to put bread through the mincer. Use fairly stale bread as fresh, doughy bread is inclined to clog the cutting knife. Citrus peel can be minced for marmalade.

Onions, other vegetables and herbs can be minced if you have no other attachments for dealing with these, see the comments page 20.

Use the mincer on a medium speed; too slow a speed encourages the food to stick round the cutting knife, too fast a speed makes it difficult to cut the food properly.

Always dismantle the mincer after use. Wash the parts in a hot detergent solution, rinse well in clear water and dry. Leave all parts at room temperature for a while to make quite certain they are absolutely dry before reassembling. Be careful that the cutting knife is stored carefully so that the blades are not distorted in any way.

4 **CHOPPING AND SLICING ATTACHMENTS** These enable you to chop (or grate or shred) and slice a variety of foods. They are fitted into the front of the mixer (*Fig 9*).

Fig 9 Chopping and slicing attachments.

You can chop or grate many vegetables, see page 79, chocolate, nuts, cheese, fresh butcher's suet, and crush biscuits.

You can shred cabbage finely with the chopping attachment, or more coarsely with the slicing attachment.

You can slice a variety of vegetables, hard fruit (such as apples) and nuts, and slice chocolate for decoration.

It is advisable to use these attachments on a medium speed. Press the food in the feed-tube down firmly, but not too vigorously, with the pusher.

Dismantle these attachments after use. Wash in hot detergent solution, rinse well in clear water and dry. Leave all parts at room temperature for a while to make quite certain they are dry.

5 **COFFEE GRINDER** Many people have ruined the blades of a blender by using it to grind coffee. The coffee grinder is an ideal investment, for you can grind the beans just before making the coffee.

Most modern coffee grinders give variable grinding, so select the position that produces just the kind of coffee you require. You can use fine-ground coffee for the jug or saucepan method but medium-ground coffee is generally recommended for use with most percolators and filter-type coffee makers. The coffee grinder is used on a medium to medium fast speed.

Never wash the grinder; simply wipe the outside with a damp cloth.

6 **COLANDER AND SIEVE** Although a blender produces a very acceptable purée of fruits and vegetables there will be times when an absolutely smooth purée is required, free from pips, fruit stones and pieces of skin. This attachment saves pushing food through a hand sieve after blending.

15

Follow the manufacturer's instructions for assembling the attachment. Use the lowest speed at first; the paddle automatically pushes the food through the selected sieve into the colander bowl, leaving the stones of fruit such as apricots, and residue, behind. You may be able to raise the speed slightly after some seconds when the mixture becomes a little stiffer and will not splash.

The various parts of the attachment must be washed very carefully and thoroughly in hot detergent solution so that the sieves do not become clogged with left-over pips, etc. Rinse well in clear water and dry.

7 **JUICE EXTRACTOR AND JUICE SEPARATOR** Do not be confused between these two attachments. You can obtain both to fit some mixers and some food processors. Follow the manufacturer's directions for assembling, using and cleaning them. Clean carefully after use.

Fig 10 A typical juice extractor.

Fig 11 A typical juice separator.

A *juice extractor* (*Fig 10*) takes the juice out of citrus fruits. It works in exactly the same way as a hand squeezer except that when fitted to the mixer or processor the electric motor gives it greater power, and more juice is extracted than when squeezing by hand. It is worth investing in this if you use a lot of citrus fruit juice. Use a medium speed when the device is part of a mixer; hold the halved fruit very firmly over the reamer. (You may well find it quicker to use a hand squeezer if a recipe requires the juice of just half a lemon or orange.)

A *juice separator* (*Fig 11*), however, is a much more elaborate piece of equipment. Its purpose is to separate the juice from the solid matter of fruits and vegetables and enables you to make your own tomato juice, carrot juice, etc. This appliance is widely acclaimed by people who follow health food diets and would be invaluable when any roughage must be avoided.

Do not try to work with too large a quantity at one time; check the manufacturer's recommendations. If there is excessive vibration or a deep droning noise it is not a matter for alarm, simply an indication that the pulped fruit or vegetables are unevenly distributed. Switch off the machine and remove the pulp or re-distribute it.

Specialist attachments

1 *Can opener* This fits in the front of the mixer and opens most cans.
2 *Bean and citrus peel slicer* Beans must first be stringed before slicing. The rind of citrus fruit is sliced more evenly than when put through the mincer attachment.
3 *Potato peeler* This rubs away the skins of new or old potatoes. It is most efficient when used with uniformly-sized small potatoes.
4 *Sausage filler* This is attached to the mincer and forms sausage shapes as the finely minced meat comes through the plate. If you can obtain sausage skins from a butcher, fit these over the sausage-making attachment.
5 *Wheat mill* This enables you to grind wheat grains at home and produce wholemeal flour. You can also grind lentils, brown or white rice. Assemble the wheat mill as the directions given by the manufacturer.

It is advisable to process the wheat at maximum speed.

Never immerse the body of the wheat mill in water, but the hopper (the container for the wheat), and the chute (through which the flour is delivered), can be washed, rinsed and dried as other attachments.

CHAPTER 2

INTERESTING DRINKS

You can make some unusual and refreshing drinks from punches to milk shakes and lemonade with the aid of some of the mixer equipment covered in this book.

Drinks using a juice extractor and separator are described on page 19.

A blender is ideal for making many drinks for the ingredients are perfectly mixed. Remember the liquid will rise quite drastically in the goblet, so only half fill this and switch gradually to maximum speed.

If you do not possess a blender you can combine the ingredients with the help of a mixer, although you will have to sieve or mash the fruit first for a fruit milk shake. A small portable electric mixer is more suitable than a large machine – put the ingredients into a large jug or really deep basin to minimize splashing. Use the mixer at the lowest speed at first and then increase to maximum. Hold the whisk(s) so they are covered by liquid; this also minimizes splashing.

A food processor is not as good as a blender for preparing drinks, but can be utilized for this purpose. If you are combining fresh fruits with milk, as the drinks described overleaf, then select the double-bladed cutting knife to make a smooth purée of the fruit. If you are simply combining ice cream or eggs with liquid, use the plastic knife, if supplied. Pour the liquid through the feed-tube with the machine in operation to avoid any possibility of the liquid splashing; never over-fill the bowl, see comments on page 14. When pouring the drink out of the processor bowl be careful the liquid does not run through the centre hole.

Iced drinks

Never use whole ice cubes when mixing drinks in a blender or food processor, or with a mixer. The solid lumps of ice could harm the blades of the blender or processor or bend the wires of a whisk. Crush the ice first as described on page 11.

Simple punches

BLACKCURRANT PUNCH: To each 300 ml ($\frac{1}{2}$ pt) sweet cider allow 2 tablespoons fresh blackcurrants, 1 tablespoon orange juice and a little sugar. If using cold cider you will need a little crushed ice, see page 11.

Blend, process or mix together the blackcurrants, orange juice and sugar, then add the hot or cold cider. For the method of combining the ingredients, see Citrus Punch.

CITRUS PUNCH: To each 300 ml ($\frac{1}{2}$ pt) white wine or dry cider use the rind of $\frac{1}{4}$ orange, $\frac{1}{4}$ lemon, 1 tablespoon orange juice and $\frac{1}{2}$ tablespoon lemon juice.

The blender or food processor must be used for this drink.

Cut away just the 'zest' (the top part of the rind), squeeze out the juice with an extractor or hand lemon squeezer.

B Put the fruit rinds into the goblet with the fruit juice, sugar and heated wine or cider. Put on the lid and switch on until the rinds are completely chopped and smooth.

FP Place the double-bladed cutting knife and bowl in position. Add the fruit rinds, fruit juice and sugar, fix the lid and switch on for a few seconds until the rinds are finely chopped. Pour the heated wine or cider through the feed-tube with the machine in operation.

STRAWBERRY GINGER PUNCH To each 300 ml ($\frac{1}{2}$ pt) ginger beer or ginger ale allow about 4 large strawberries and sugar to taste. Blend, process or mix the ingredients together, see Citrus Punch. Serve cold.

OLD FASHIONED LEMONADE

Halve the lemons and remove any pips. To each 2 lemons allow 600 ml (1 pt) water and approximately 50 g (2 oz) sugar or 2 tablespoons honey.

B Cut the halved lemons into pieces. Put into the blender goblet with the sugar or honey. Heat the water and pour on to the lemons. Fix the lid and switch on until the lemons are finely chopped. Pour into a jug; allow the drink to cool. Strain and dilute with more water or with soda water.

FP Cut the halved lemons into pieces. Place the double-bladed cutting knife and bowl in position. Add the lemon with the sugar or honey, fix the lid and switch on for a few seconds until the lemons are finely chopped. Heat the water and pour through the feed-tube with the machine in operation. Pour into a jug; allow the drink to cool. Strain and dilute with more water or with soda water.

To vary
Oranges can be used in the same way, but substitute 3 oranges for 2 lemons.

Milk shakes

The combination of hot or cold milk and flavouring is an excellent way of producing a nourishing, as well as delicious, beverage. Often children who dislike 'plain milk' will enjoy a fluffy, flavoured milk drink. Below are some of the ways in which a milk shake can be made. It is not easy to blend acid fruits and milk except with the high speed of a blender or food processor, and even when using these appliances you should be careful that the milk is not actually at boiling point when it is mixed with the fruit for a hot milk shake. Do not allow the cold milk and fruit to stand in the blender goblet or bowl of the food processor before emulsifying them together.

Fresh fruit milk shakes
Any fresh fruit can be used, but some of the most interesting are halved bananas, stoned ripe apricots, blackberries, blackcurrants, stoned ripe cherries, raspberries, strawberries and other soft fruit, oranges (discard pips, pith and skin) and sliced skinned peaches.

Allow the equivalent of 2 tablespoons fruit or half a banana or peach to each 300 ml ($\frac{1}{2}$ pt) milk.

HOT FRUIT MILK SHAKES

B Put the fruit into the blender goblet and add any sugar required. Pour on the hot, but not boiling, milk, put on the lid and switch on immediately.

M Mash or sieve the fruit and put into a jug or basin. Heat the milk and add a little sugar to this if desired. Pour the milk on to the fruit, whisking as you do so.

FP Place the double-bladed cutting knife and bowl in position. Add the fruit and sugar, fix the lid and switch on for a few seconds until a smooth purée. Pour the hot, but not boiling, milk gradually through the feed-tube with the machine in operation.

COLD FRUIT MILK SHAKES

Proceed as for hot milk shakes, but add a little crushed ice to the fruit, or a spoonful of vanilla or other flavoured ice cream, if liked. This makes sure the drink is really ice cold.

To vary
There are many other ways of preparing milk shakes, e.g. flavour with various ice creams; add strong coffee or instant coffee powder; cocoa or chocolate powder.

Use the flavoured syrups which are available today.

Add fruit-flavoured liqueurs such as apricot or cherry brandy.

Make a savoury milk shake by adding a little yeast extract or very well-flavoured stock.

EGG NOGS

To each 200 ml ($\frac{1}{3}$ pt) milk allow 1 egg and 1– 2 tablespoons sherry or brandy or whisky. Mix the ingredients as described under Milk Shakes. The milk is usually heated, but an ice cold Egg Nog is delicious.

CHAPTER 3

HORS D'OEUVRE

A good starter is important; it 'sets the tone' of a meal. It can turn a fairly hum-drum family meal into a more exciting one.
It is very easy to prepare a variety of hors d'oeuvre with the help of the blender, some of the mixer attachments or a food processor.

Home-made pâtés are delicious; once upon a time they were difficult and time-consuming to prepare. Nowadays, with modern equipment, they are quick and easy.

Fruit and vegetable cocktails

If you have a juice separator (page 16) make use of this for interesting and refreshing drinks, or use the juice to pour over raw fruits.

Follow the directions given by the manufacturer for extracting the juice; there are also brief hints on page 16.

CARROT AND ORANGE COCKTAIL Blend equal quantities of carrot and orange juice. (You may find it easier to use the juice extractor for the oranges.)

CARROT AND TOMATO COCKTAIL Blend together one third carrot and two-thirds tomato juice. Flavour as suggested in the Tomato Juice Cocktail below.

CARROT, ONION AND TOMATO SALAD
Extract the juice from several carrots and 1–2 onions. Slice raw tomatoes and arrange on a bed of lettuce. Mix the vegetable juices, season with celery salt, paprika and a little cayenne pepper. Spoon over the tomatoes. Sprinkle with chopped chives.

TOMATO JUICE COCKTAIL Freshly made tomato juice makes a delicious start to a meal. Choose really ripe tomatoes. Chill the juice and flavour with a little dry sherry, Worcestershire sauce, a few drops of Tabasco sauce or crushed mint leaves. Season with celery or garlic salt and pepper.

Fish cocktails

The slicing attachment of a mixer or slicing disc of a food processor (page 15) gives the thin strips of lettuce necessary for fish cocktails. Wash, dry and cut the lettuce into 6 – 8 portions, then put through the slicing attachment. Spoon into glasses.

The Mayonnaise Dressings suggested are on pages 71–72.

ANCHOVY AND WHITE FISH COCKTAIL
Cook and dice white fish. Marinate the fish in Anchovy Mayonnaise for 1 hour. Skin and dice tomatoes, and slice a little celery. Stir the tomatoes and celery gently into the fish mixture. Spoon over the shredded lettuce. Garnish with chopped hard-boiled egg.

PRAWN AND MELON COCKTAIL Make the Lemon Mayonnaise. Cut the flesh of the melon into tiny balls or neat dice. Peel the prawns. Mix the prawns with the mayonnaise. Top the shredded lettuce with the prawn mixture, then a layer of melon.

SHELLFISH COCKTAIL Most shellfish can be used for this; although prawns are the most popular. Try a mixture of mussels, prawns, cockles and crabmeat for a pleasant change. Make the Mary Rose Dressing and marinate the shellfish in this. You can also add finely sliced celery and/ or red or green pepper, diced dessert apple. Top the shredded lettuce with the shellfish mixture. Garnish with lemon wedges.

Preparing pâtés

Pâtés vary considerably both in the ingredients used and in the method of preparation.

In the recipes on pages 22–23 the meat and fish mixtures are prepared, then placed into the oven to set. It is important that the pâtés are cooked slowly and that the dish is placed in a 'bain-marie' (tin or dish of cold water) so that the pâté keeps moist during cooking. In this type of pâté use a food processor or mincer attachment to chop or mince the raw meat or fish. A blender is less successful for this purpose.

In the second group of recipes, which begin on page 21, the raw or cooked ingredients are blended together to produce a smooth pâté. The food processor, blender or mincer attachment can be used as described below.

Pâtés using the mincer attachment

Cut raw meat or raw fish into neat dice; discard any bones, gristle or skin. Feed the food into the mincer with the motor running at medium speed. If you require a very smooth fine mixture, mince the ingredients twice and select the finest mincing plate (screen), if you have a choice of sizes. When the recipe contains meat or fish, with peeled onion(s) and bread, mince the ingredients in this order. By mincing the bread last the excess juices from the onion and meat or fish are absorbed by the bread.

Cooked meat or fish are minced in the same way. It is not satisfactory to put liquid, cream or sauces through the mincer, the final blending should be done by hand.

Pâtés using the food processor

Cut raw meat or fish into neat dice, discard any bones, gristle or skin. Place the double-bladed cutting knife and bowl in position. Add the meat or fish, fix the lid and switch on to chop the food finely. The peeled onion(s) and other ingredients can be added to the meat or fish so the mixture is evenly chopped and then blended. Remember the food processor chops within seconds so do not leave the motor running for too long a period.

When blending cooked ingredients or those that do not require cooking – as in the Smoked Fish Pâté on page 22, put all the ingredients together into the bowl, using the double-bladed cutting knife. Switch on for a few seconds only until the pâté is as fine as required. If you want a pâté in which there are larger pieces of one or more foods, blended with the smoother mixture, as in the Ham and Tongue Pâté on page 63, drop the diced meat through the feed-tube and allow about 1– 2 seconds only. In this way you will produce the interesting variation of textures.

It is not necessary to melt the butter or other fat when preparing a pâté in a food processor.

Pâtés using the blender

Although cooked pâté ingredients (or those that do not require cooking) can be blended, it is not recommended that you try to chop raw meat, except tender liver or fish, in a blender.

It is important to appreciate that only small quantities are blended together at one time. Put in the ingredients, switch on until well blended, then transfer from the goblet to a mixing bowl. Add more pâté ingredients, switch on again. Continue in batches until all the pâté is prepared. The time taken to blend each batch of pâté will be a few seconds only.

You will find the meat, or other pâté, mixture is easier to blend if the butter, or other fat, is melted. This will make the pâté mixture appear over-soft in texture, but it will thicken as the fat cools.

Freezing pâtés

Advice is given under the various recipes as to the approximate time for freezing the mixture. Pâtés cannot be frozen for a long period as the mixture tends to become dry and less palatable.

TURKEY PÂTÉ

Serves 4–6
Cooking time 10 mins
Use Mincer Attachment of Mixer, Blender
or Food Processor

2 eggs
225 g (8 oz) cooked turkey
4 small cocktail onions
2 tablespoons double cream
3 tablespoons mayonnaise
salt and pepper
1 teaspoon French mustard

1   Hard-boil the eggs and shell. Dice the turkey meat.

(MA) 2   Put the turkey through the mincer, then the onions. Coarsely chop the eggs with a knife. Blend all the ingredients together in a mixing bowl.

(B)   Put the turkey into the blender goblet with the rest of the ingredients, except the eggs. Switch on until smooth. Spoon into a mixing bowl. Coarsely chop the eggs and stir into the turkey mixture.

(FP)   Place the double-bladed cutting knife and bowl in position. Put the turkey and the rest of the ingredients, except the eggs, into the bowl. Fix the lid and switch on for a few seconds until almost smooth. Drop the eggs through the feed-tube with the motor in operation.

3   Serve the pâté with hot toast and butter.

To freeze
Do not freeze this or any dish containing hard-boiled eggs.

To vary
Cooked chicken or game birds can be used instead of turkey in any of these recipes.

TURKEY AND HAM PÂTÉ: Use 100 g (4 oz) cooked ham instead of eggs.

TURKEY AND TONGUE PÂTÉ: Use 100 g (4 oz) cooked tongue instead of eggs.

TURKEY AND CHEESE PÂTÉ: Use 225 g (8 oz) cream or cottage cheese instead of eggs.

TURKEY AND SHERRY PÂTÉ: Omit the mayonnaise; use 50 g (2 oz) melted butter and 2 tablespoons dry sherry.

CHEESE AND EGG PÂTÉ: Follow the basic recipe but use diced Cheddar cheese instead of turkey.

Speedy pâtés and dips

The following recipes are all based on mixtures prepared in the blender or food processor, using the double-bladed cutting knife. You will need to liquidize the mixture in several batches when using a blender.

These pâtés, usually served with hot toast and butter, are equally good as a dip. To serve as a dip, put the mixture into a bowl, place crisp strips of celery and carrot, savoury biscuits, potato crisps etc. on a tray around the bowl to dip. Recipes serve 4–6. See also page 64 for more dips.

AUBERGINE PÂTÉ Bake 2 large aubergines for about 1 hour in a cool oven, 150°C, 300°F, Gas Mark 2, until very soft. Halve the aubergines and scoop out the pulp. Peel 1 small onion, put in the blender goblet or bowl of the food processor with the aubergine pulp, $\frac{1}{2}$ tablespoon lemon juice, salt and pepper to taste; switch on until smooth.
You can add a little Worcestershire sauce or Tabasco sauce to flavour.

AVOCADO PÂTÉ Skin and quarter 2 large tomatoes, put into the blender goblet or bowl of the food processor with a sprig of parsley, 2 small spring onions and 1 tablespoon lemon juice. Switch on until smooth. Halve 2 ripe avocados and scoop out the pulp. Stir into the tomato mixture with a few drops of Tabasco sauce. You can add the avocado pulp to the mixture in the blender or food processor, but it does tend to make a softer mixture.

SMOKED SALMON DIP Dice about 175 g (6 oz) smoked salmon pieces. Melt 75 g (3 oz) butter. Put the butter, smoked salmon, 150 ml ($\frac{1}{4}$ pt) single cream, 1 tablespoon tomato purée, 2 tablespoons lemon juice, shake paprika and pepper in the blender goblet or bowl of the food processor. Switch on until smooth.

SPEEDY LIVER PÂTÉ Put 225 g (8 oz) liver sausage, 100–175 g (4–6 oz) cottage cheese, 25 g (1 oz) halved walnuts, 2 tablespoons cream, salt, pepper and a few drops Worcestershire sauce in the blender goblet or bowl of the food processor. Switch on until smooth.

21

SMOKED TROUT PÂTÉ

Serves 4–6

Cooking time 1 min
Use Juice Extractor Attachment of Mixer
and Blender or Juice Extractor Attachment
of Food Processor and Food Processor

1 large lemon
40 g (1½ oz) butter
3 large smoked trout
1–2 cloves garlic
3–5 tablespoons single cream*
1 tablespoon horseradish cream
salt and pepper
cayenne pepper
To garnish
lettuce, lemon slices
*Depending on how thick you like the pâté

MA
OR
FP
1 Fix the juice extractor, halve the lemon
and extract the juice; or use a hand
squeezer – you need approximately 2
tablespoons.

2 Melt the butter. (It is not essential to
melt the butter when using a food
processor, but make sure it is softened.)
Remove all the flesh from the fish,
discarding the bones and skin. Peel the
garlic.

B 3 Put some of the lemon juice, butter and
cream into the blender goblet, add
some of the fish, horseradish cream and
seasonings (be sparing with the salt and
cayenne pepper). Switch on until
blended; remove with the plastic
scraper supplied by the manufacturer.
Blend the next batch of ingredients and
continue in batches until all the pâté is
prepared.

FP Place the double-bladed cutting knife
and bowl in position. Add all the
ingredients, fix the lid and switch on for
a few seconds.

4 Chill the pâté; as the butter sets the
pâté will stiffen. Serve with hot toast and
butter and garnish with lettuce and
lemon slices.

To freeze
This pâté freezes well if used within 3–4
weeks.

To vary
SMOKED MACKEREL PÂTÉ Use 2 smoked
mackerel instead of trout.

SMOKED SALMON PÂTÉ Use
approximately 100 g (4 oz) smoked salmon

instead of trout; most fishmongers sell
smoked salmon pieces more cheaply than
sliced salmon. Omit the horseradish and
salt.

SMOKED EEL PÂTÉ Use approximately
100 g (4 oz) smoked eel instead of trout and
2 teaspoons tomato purée (this gives the
pâté a delicate colour).

TARAMASALATA Use 100–175 g (4–6 oz)
skinned smoked cod's roe instead of the
trout. Omit the horseradish and salt.

SMOKED HADDOCK PÂTÉ Poach a
smoked haddock or haddock fillets in
water or milk until tender. Flake the fish
from the skin and bones. Use 225 g (8 oz)
fish, 50 g (2 oz) melted butter, 1–2
tablespoons lemon juice, 1 peeled clove
garlic, pepper to taste and 4–5 tablespoons
single cream. A few fennel or dill leaves
and small sprig of parsley can be blended
or processed with the other ingredients.

Cooked kippers, bloaters or buckling
can be used instead of haddock.

WHITE FISH PÂTÉ Poached white fish
makes a delicate pâté but it needs extra
flavouring. Poach the fish in white wine or
add a peeled and chopped onion to the
liquid in which the fish is cooked. To
225–300 g (8–10 oz) cooked fish allow 50 g
(2 oz) butter, 4 tablespoons double cream,
1 tablespoon dry sherry and 1–2
tablespoons lemon juice. A little anchovy
essence can be added to give extra flavour,
in which case be sparing with the salt.
Fennel or dill leaves, parsley or chives and
stuffed olives can all be blended or
processed with the fish.

Based upon Pâté de Foie

TERRINE OF HERBS Follow the instructions
for the Pâté de Foie, but mince or process
2 peeled onions, 2 peeled cloves garlic, 1
small sprig of basil, parsley, rosemary, a
few sorrel and tarragon leaves with the
liver.

TERRINE OF CHICKEN Remove the flesh
from a raw chicken, plus the liver, to give
approximately 450 g (1 lb). Skin and use
instead of the pig's liver. Mince or process
a sprig of parsley, rosemary and thyme
with the chicken and bacon or belly of
pork. Mince or process 1 peeled medium
onion separately. Heat 50 g (2 oz) butter in
a pan. Fry the onion for a few minutes then
blend with the other ingredients.

TERRINE OF DUCK Use the flesh from 1 or 2 raw duckling(s) plus the liver(s). Skin and use instead of the pig's liver – you need approximately 675 g (1½ lb) duck flesh to use the proportions of liquid etc. in the basic recipe. Omit the bacon or pork. Mince or process several sage leaves, the 'zest' (top orange part of the peel) from 1 orange, 2 peeled cloves garlic with the duck. Use duck stock made by simmering the bones of the bird(s) instead of beef stock and cream. A peeled medium onion can also be minced or processed with the duck meat.

You can omit some of the stock and substitute the same amount of orange juice.

PÂTÉ DE FOIE

This pâté does not have a pastry case or a coating of bacon, making it particularly easy to prepare. Often this type of pâté is given the name 'terrine'.

Serves 6–8
Cooking time 1½ hours
Use Mincer Attachment of Mixer *or* Food Processor

450 g (1 lb) pig's liver
225 g (8 oz) fat bacon (weight without rinds) or fat belly of pork (weight without skin)
4 tablespoons beef stock
150 ml (¼ pt) double cream
2 eggs
salt and pepper

1   Cut the liver and bacon or pork into 2.5–4-cm (1–1½-in) dice.
2   For a rough-textured pâté select the coarse plate (screen). Feed the meats through the hopper, pressing down gently with the pusher. Do not push too hard for this makes the blood run too much from the raw liver. For a smooth textured pâté use the fine plate and mince the meats twice. Blend the minced meats with the other ingredients.
Place the double-bladed cutting knife and bowl in position. Add about a third of the meats, fix the lid, switch on and process until the mixture is as fine as wanted. Remember you need only about 4–5 seconds for a coarse cut pâté and about 10 seconds for a finely cut, smooth pâté. Transfer the chopped meats to a mixing bowl; repeat with half the remaining meats and then with the rest of the meats. Mix with the other ingredients.

3   Butter a 1-kg (2-lb) loaf tin, ovenproof mould or terrine mould. Put in the mixture and cover with buttered foil; stand in a tin (bain-marie) with cold water coming half-way up the sides of the mould.
4   Bake in the centre of a moderate oven, 160°C, 325°F, Gas Mark 3, for 1½ hours.
5   Put a light weight on the pâté as it cools.
6   Serve with hot toast and butter.

To freeze
This pâté freezes well for up to 1 month.

To vary
Peel 1–2 medium onions and 1–2 cloves garlic; mince or chop with the liver.
For a more delicate flavour use calf's or lamb's liver.

BRANDY PÂTÉ Use only 2 tablespoons stock and 2 tablespoons brandy.

CHICKEN LIVER PÂTÉ Use 450 g (1 lb) uncooked chicken's liver in the basic recipe or any of the variations.

ECONOMICAL PÂTÉ Use a thick sauce made with 25 g (1 oz) butter, margarine or chicken fat, 25 g (1 oz) flour, 150 ml (¼ pt) milk instead of the cream.

LIVER AND CHEESE PÂTÉ Omit the cream and mix with 225 g (8 oz) cream cheese.

SMOKED HADDOCK MOUSSE

(Illustrated on page 33)

Serves 8
Cooking time 30 mins
Use Juice Extractor Attachment of Mixer, Blender and Mixer *or* Juice Extractor Attachment of Food Processor and Food Processor

1 lemon
2 eggs
450 g (1 lb) smoked haddock (weight without skin and bones)
300 ml (½ pt) milk (see stage 4)
25 g (1 oz) butter
20 g (¾ oz) flour
2 tablespoons water
15 g (½ oz) powdered gelatine
300 ml (½ pt) mayonnaise
pepper
150 ml (¼ pt) double cream
salt (optional)

To garnish
stuffed green olives

MA 1 Fix the juice extractor, halve the lemon
OR   and extract the juice; or use a hand
FP   squeezer – you need approximately 2
      tablespoons.

2 Hard-boil the eggs, shell and chop.

3 Put the haddock and milk into an
     ovenproof dish and cover with foil or a
     lid. Place just above the centre of a
     moderately hot oven, 190°C, 375°F, Gas
     Mark 5, for about 20 minutes.

4 Drain and flake the fish. Retain the milk,
     measure and add a little more milk to
     make 300 ml (½ pt) again.

5 Melt the butter in a saucepan, stir in the
     flour and cook over a low heat for 2
     minutes. Gradually blend in the milk,
     stirring as the sauce comes to the boil
     and thickens.

6 Meanwhile, put the water into a bowl,
     sprinkle the gelatine on top. Stand the
     bowl over a pan of boiling water until
     the gelatine has dissolved. Stir the
     gelatine mixture into the hot sauce.

7 Mix the sauce, cooked haddock,
     mayonnaise, a shake of pepper and the
     lemon juice together.

B 8 Spoon some of this mixture into the
     blender goblet, switch on until quite
     smooth, then put into a mixing bowl (do
     not use the bowl of the mixer, see stage
     9); continue in batches until all the fish
     mixture has been blended.

FP   Place the double-bladed cutting knife
     and bowl in position. Add all the fish
     mixture (or as much as the capacity of
     the bowl will allow), fix the lid and
     switch on for a few seconds until the
     mixture is smooth.

M 9 Pour the cream into the mixer bowl and
     whisk on low speed until the cream just
     holds its shape; fold the cream into the
     fish mixture.

FP   A food processor will not whip cream,
     so a hand whisk could be used.

10 Lastly add the chopped hard-boiled
     eggs. Taste the mixture, add a little
     more pepper and salt if necessary.
     Spoon the mixture into 8 individual
     dishes; leave to set.

11 Slice the olives by hand and arrange on
     top of the mousse. Serve with toast and
     butter.

To freeze
This mousse freezes well for 6 weeks.

To vary
Serves 4 as a main dish with salad.

SALMON MOUSSE

This is a very simple basic recipe that
could be used with most fish. The dish
serves 8 as an hors d'oeuvre.

Put 3 tablespoons white wine, dry
vermouth or fish stock, made as page 46
(and flavoured with lemon juice), into a
large bowl. Add 15 g (½ oz) gelatine and
place over boiling water to dissolve the
gelatine. Add a few drops Tabasco sauce,
1–2 teaspoons tomato purée, 300 ml (½ pt/10
fl oz) natural yogurt, 3 tablespoons thick
mayonnaise and approximately 450 g (1 lb)
flaked cooked or canned salmon. Whisk 2
egg whites in the mixer or food processor –
if the type of processor that does whisk egg
whites. Fold into the salmon mixture, add
salt and pepper to taste. Spoon into an
oiled mould; leave to set. This mousse will
freeze well for 6 weeks.

CHAPTER 4
SOUPS

Several appliances will be an asset when preparing vegetables for soups; you can use

a) The chopping, slicing or mincer attachments of a mixer.

b) The blender.

c) The chopping or slicing attachments of a food processor, or the double-bladed metal cutting knife.

These produce finely chopped or thinly sliced vegetables, see page 26, also pages 79 and 81.

You save cooking time and fuel when the vegetables are in small pieces. The soup has a better flavour and colour because the cooking time is so short.

Soups using the blender

Warm glass blender goblets before adding the very hot soup. I generally hold the upturned goblet over the pan of hot soup for a short time.

Always check that there are no tiny pieces of bone (from meat or poultry) in the soup before adding it to the goblet. Always check that the base of the goblet is screwed on tightly, see page 11.

Pour or spoon the solid ingredients and liquid into the goblet. The liquid content makes the mixture rise in the goblet when the motor is switched on so it is imperative to see that

a) The goblet is only half-filled.

b) The lid is securely fixed.

Switch on until the mixture is as smooth as desired. In most cases you have a perfectly smooth purée, even when pieces of cooked poultry, fish or meat are included.

You may, however, find that some hard pips, particles of tomato skin or pieces of cooked celery are not completely puréed. This may not matter, but if you want a completely smooth soup sieve the puréed mixture. Although this is an extra job, it is surprisingly easy once the soup has been liquidized.

Adding herbs If you want chopped herbs in the soup, add sprigs of parsley, etc. when the mixture is almost smooth. Switch off the machine, remove the lid, or cap in the lid, add the herbs, replace the lid or cap and switch on again. In this way you avoid any possibility of being splashed by the very hot soup.

Note With many blenders you may well find that the very hot, or almost boiling, soup tends to create a vacuum in the goblet and makes it very difficult to remove the lid, especially if the lid is left in position for any length of time. Always move the lid – or cap in the lid – the moment after you switch off.

Soups using the food processor

The general principle of preparing a puréed soup is similar in both the blender and food processor, with one important difference. You will achieve a better result if you spoon the solid pieces of cooked vegetables, meat, poultry, etc. out of the soup and place them into the food processor bowl with the double-bladed metal cutting knife in position. Add a few tablespoons only of liquid. Fix the lid and switch on until a smooth purée. Either add this to the soup liquid remaining in the saucepan or add the liquid gradually through the feed-tube of the food processor. Switch on to blend.

Never over-fill the food processor bowl for the liquid mixture will spill out through the join between the bowl and lid.

Thickening soups

You will notice that in many recipes in this book relatively little flour or cornflour is used. One advantage of using a blender or food processor is that the basic ingredients act as the natural thickener. Obviously, root vegetables, such as potatoes, are particularly good.

If you are on a low carbohydrate diet you avoid using flour or cornflour and still have an excellent thickened soup.

If using flour or cornflour for thickening the soup, add to the last batch of purée in the blender or food processor, then switch on until absorbed. Naturally, you will need to return the mixture to the saucepan, bring the soup to boiling point and allow it to boil, or simmer (depending upon the ingredients used) until the flour or cornflour loses its uncooked taste. Stir during this stage.

Vegetable soups
These soups are so easily prepared that you can prepare enough soup for a meal in minutes, or cook larger quantities, enjoy some the same day and freeze the remainder. Imagine serving home-made fresh pea or asparagus soup in the middle of winter.

Pack soup for freezing in relatively small polythene boxes, cartons or freezer-type polythene bags (supported in cartons until the semi-liquid mixture has formed a neat, solid block). You can then take the bag out of the carton, label and pack it away.

The information on this and the previous page about preparing soups will be helpful in selecting and using the appliance correctly.

You will also find advice on preparing vegetables for cooking on pages 79 to 81.

Briefly, there are three ways in which vegetables are prepared for soup, i.e.
a) The vegetables are chopped *before* making the soup, and the soup is served with pieces of vegetables in the liquid; examples of this type of soup are on pages 28 and 31. Finely chopped vegetables cook more quickly and so retain flavour and texture. Some people find that onions chopped before cooking and then put into the liquid for soup are less mellow than if they are chopped and tossed in fat first.
b) The vegetables are chopped before cooking, then the soup is blended or processed into a smooth purée, as the recipes on pages 28 and 32.
c) The whole vegetables are cooked, then chopped or puréed, see the recipes on pages 35 and 36.

Cold soups
Some soups based upon vegetables are delicious cold, see pages 28 and 29.

Dealing with large quantities of soup
Do not over-fill the blender goblet or bowl of the food processor, see details on filling the appliances pages 11 and 14. Blend or process some of the mixture, transfer to a second saucepan or the warmed mixing bowl. Continue in batches until all the soup is puréed.

To stop soups separating in freezing
Soups prepared in the blender or food processor have less tendency to separate or become thinner in consistency in freezing, since the mixtures depend less upon flour or cornflour thickening.

If the recipe does contain flour or cornflour, use an extra teaspoon. Blend this with about 2 tablespoons liquid (stock or milk, etc. depending upon the recipe).

Pour the soup into the container, spoon the blended flour or cornflour on top. When reheating the soup, stir in the extra thickening as the sauce warms through.

GARBURE

Serves 6–8
Cooking time 1½–1¾ hours
Use Blender *or* Food Processor

50–75 g (2–3 oz) haricot beans
water (see method)
1 medium carrot
¼–½ medium turnip
1 medium potato
1–2 medium onions
1 large or 2 small leeks
1–2 sticks celery from the heart
about ¼ small cabbage heart
2 rashers streaky bacon
50 g (2 oz) butter or margarine
bouquet garni
salt and pepper
To garnish
chopped parsley

1 Put the haricot beans into a bowl, cover with 1.2 litres (2 pt) cold water and leave for at least 5 hours to soak.
2 Put the beans and water into a saucepan, cover tightly and simmer for 1 hour.
3 Peel the root vegetables and onion(s). Wash the leeks, discard the top tough green part. Wash the celery and cabbage.

4 Chop all the vegetables roughly into pieces about 2.5 cm (1 in) in size. Measure out a generous 300 ml (½ pt) water to use in stage 5.

B 5 Put some of the vegetables and water into the blender goblet, switch on until finely chopped, see advice on page 25. Continue in batches until all the vegetables including the cabbage, are neatly chopped. Strain after chopping but retain the 300 ml (½ pt) water, see stage 7. Blot the vegetables dry with absorbent paper.

FP Place the double-bladed cutting knife and bowl in position. Add some of the vegetables, fix the lid and switch on to chop them, see advice on page 25. Continue in batches. Do not add any liquid.

6 De-rind the bacon, cut into neat matchstick pieces with kitchen scissors, put into a large saucepan and fry for a few minutes until crisp. Remove and put on one side.

7 Heat the butter or margarine in the saucepan used for frying the bacon; add the chopped vegetables and toss in the butter for a few minutes; add the 300 ml (½ pt) liquid together with the haricot beans and liquid in which they were cooked. (This should have been reduced to 750 ml (1¼ pt).)

8 Add the bouquet garni, salt and pepper to taste. Cover the pan, simmer steadily until the vegetables are tender but not over-soft.

9 Add the bacon for the last few minutes of the cooking.

10 Remove the bouquet garni. Garnish with chopped parsley and serve.

To freeze
This version can be frozen for about 1 month, but the vegetables tend to become over-soft. The first variation given below gives a better result. Add the cream when reheating.

To vary
CREAMY GARBURE Use about 150 ml (¼ pt) less liquid. When the vegetables, including beans, are tender, put into the blender goblet with the liquid, or bowl of the food processor with the minimum of liquid. Switch on until a smooth purée, return to the saucepan with the liquid, the bacon and 150 ml (¼ pt) double cream and reheat for a few minutes. Garnish with the parsley.

SPEEDY GARBURE Omit the haricot beans. Prepare the vegetables and bacon; proceed as stages 4–8. Add a small to medium sized can of haricot beans when the vegetables are nearly soft; continue as stages 9 and 10.

TOMATO GARBURE Use half water and half tomato juice or add about 4 large skinned, chopped tomatoes to the vegetable mixture.

VEGETABLE LENTIL SOUP Use 75 g (3 oz) lentils in place of haricot beans. Omit the cabbage. Soak the lentils in 1.2 litres (2 pt) water for 2 hours as stage 1; simmer for 45 minutes. Prepare and cut the vegetables as stages 3–5; chop and cook the bacon as stage 6 then continue as stages 7 and 8.

Garbure is typical of a satisfying vegetable soup. Other vegetables could be substituted or you can omit the dried beans and stages 1 and 2.

CREAMED STILTON AND ONION SOUP

(Illustrated on page 37)

Serves 4–6
Cooking time 25 mins
Use Grating Attachment of Mixer and Blender *or* Food Processor

3 medium onions
175 g (6 oz) Stilton cheese
50 g (2 oz) butter
50 g (2 oz) flour
450 ml (¾ pt) stock
450 ml (¾ pt) milk
2–4 teaspoons Worcestershire sauce (depending on personal taste)
salt and pepper
To garnish
chopped chives or parsley

1 Peel and dice the onions. Dice the cheese.

MA 2 Put the onions through the grating attachment of the mixer.

FP Place the double-bladed cutting knife and bowl in position. Add the onions, fix the lid and switch on for 2–3 seconds only; do not over-process.

3 Heat the butter in a large saucepan, add the onions and fry gently for about 5 minutes until soft.

4 Stir in the flour and cook for 1 minute.
5 Gradually add the stock and milk, stir constantly, and bring to the boil.
6 Reduce the heat and simmer for 10 minutes. Add the diced Stilton, Worcestershire sauce, a little salt and pepper and simmer for a further 5–6 minutes or until the cheese has melted.

B 7 Tip the soup into the warmed blender goblet, and switch on until smooth.

FP Using the double-bladed cutting knife, spoon the solid ingredients out of the soup into the bowl, plus a little liquid. Fix the lid and switch on until a smooth purée, then gradually add the rest of the liquid through the feed-tube.

8 Reheat gently, adding extra seasoning to taste if necessary. Garnish with chopped chives or parsley.

To freeze
This soup is best freshly made.

BOTWINJA

This Russian vegetable soup is delicious when served well chilled.

Serves 4–6
Cooking time 5–6 mins
Use Blender *or* Food Processor

175 g (6 oz) young spinach
enough sorrel to give 1 tablespoon when chopped
1.2 litres (2 pt) light ale
salt and pepper
1 small cucumber
enough chervil, chives, fennel leaves, parsley and tarragon to give 1 tablespoon each when chopped
To garnish
natural yogurt or cream

1 Wash the spinach and sorrel.

B 2 Put a little ale, the spinach and sorrel into the blender goblet. Switch on until finely chopped. Transfer to a saucepan.

FP Place the double-bladed cutting knife and bowl in position. Add some of the spinach, fix the lid and switch on until chopped finely. Transfer to a saucepan. Chop the rest of the spinach and sorrel, put into the saucepan with a little ale.

3 Add a little salt and pepper, simmer steadily for 5–6 minutes. Allow to cool.

B OR FP 4 Put the spinach mixture into the blender goblet or bowl of the food processor using the double-bladed cutting knife; switch on until puréed.

5 Peel the cucumber and cut into 2.5-cm (1-in) pieces.

B Put into the blender goblet with the herbs and a little more ale; switch on until finely chopped.

FP Place the cucumber and herbs into the bowl of the food processor, using the double-bladed cutting knife. Fix the lid and switch on until finely chopped.

6 Mix together the spinach purée, chopped cucumber, herbs and remaining light ale. Add salt and pepper to taste.

7 Chill well and serve topped with yogurt or cream.

To freeze
This soup must be freshly prepared.

To vary
Use chicken stock instead of light ale, or a mixture of chicken stock and dry white wine.

GAZPACHO

Serves 4–6
No cooking
Use Blender *or* Food Processor (See also stage 4)

75–100 g (3–4 oz) bread (weight without crusts)
550 g (1¼ lb) tomatoes
2–3 tablespoons olive oil
water (see method)
2 medium onions
2 cloves garlic
1 red pepper
1 green pepper
1 small cucumber
1 tablespoon white wine vinegar
salt and pepper

1 Break the bread into pieces.
2 To make breadcrumbs:

B Put a little bread into the dry blender goblet, cover with the lid; switch on to maximum speed until the bread becomes fine crumbs.

You can remove the centre cap from the lid, or make a foil cover with a centre hole or foil funnel and feed more bread through the hole or funnel with the machine in operation. This procedure is better with fresh doughy bread. Remove the crumbs and continue in batches until all the bread is chopped.

FP Place the double-bladed cutting knife and bowl in position. If *stale* put all the bread into the bowl, fix the lid, switch on for a few seconds. If the bread is *fresh* you will find it tends to cling to the blades of the knife. Follow the above procedure; do not put into the bowl, but fix the lid, switch on and push the bread through the feed-tube with the pusher. Do not over-process the bread.

3 Put the breadcrumbs into a small serving bowl and cover.

4 Skin the tomatoes either by putting them into boiling water for a few minutes, then into cold water, or by inserting a fine skewer into each tomato and holding it over the heated gas ring or electric hotplate until the skin cracks. Pull away the skins, halve the tomatoes, remove the seeds (this process is known as 'concassing'). If preferred simply rub the unskinned tomatoes through the sieve and colander attachment of a mixer.

B OR FP 5 Put the tomatoes, oil and 1 tablespoon water into the blender goblet or bowl of the food processor, using the double-bladed cutting knife. Switch on until a smooth purée, leave in the goblet or food processor bowl.

6 Peel and halve the onions and peel the garlic. Halve the peppers, discard the core and seeds. Peel and roughly slice half the cucumber.

B 7 Remove the cap from the blender lid or use a foil lid or funnel. Switch on the blender to medium speed and gradually add half an onion, all the garlic, half a green and half a red pepper and the sliced cucumber to the tomato mixture; leave running until a smooth mixture.

FP Switch on and press the vegetables, as above, through the feed-tube with the pusher. Leave running for about 30 seconds or until a smooth purée.

8 Tip the tomato mixture into a bowl, add sufficient water to make a flowing consistency, and flavour with the vinegar, salt and pepper. Chill well.

B OR FP 9 Wash and dry the blender goblet or food processor bowl and cutting knife. Chop the remaining 1½ onions in the blender or food processor and put into a small serving dish. Chop the remaining pepper halves and put into a second serving dish. Peel and dice the remaining cucumber by hand and put into a serving dish.

10 Serve the Gazpacho in a large tureen with the bowls of breadcrumbs, onion, peppers and cucumber around.

To freeze
The smooth tomato and vegetable purée freezes well for up to 6 months.

FRENCH ONION SOUP

The secret of this simple soup is that the onions must be thinly sliced, then cut into neat pieces so they are easy to eat. Select the slicing attachment·or disc that gives the thinnest slices. The stock must be really well flavoured and free from excess fat.

Serves 4–6
Cooking time 25 mins
Use Slicing Attachment of Mixer *or* Slicing Disc of Food Processor

550 g (1¼ lb) onions
50 g (2 oz) butter
1·2 litres (2 pt) beef stock
1–2 bay leaves
1 sprig fresh thyme
salt and pepper

1　Peel the onions. If the onions are large cut into quarters, if small cut into halves. The pieces must fit into the feed-tube of the slicing disc of the food processor.
2　Fix the slicing attachment or disc; press the onions through with the pusher.
3　Heat the butter in a saucepan, add the onions and fry gently until golden; do not allow to discolour.
4　Add the stock, bay leaves, thyme and salt and pepper to taste. Cover the pan and simmer gently for 15 minutes or until the onions are soft but not over-cooked.
5　Remove the bay leaves and thyme before serving.

To freeze
This soup freezes well for up to 3 months.

To vary
Add 1 or 2 peeled and sliced cloves garlic to the onions in the basic recipe or variations given below.

CREAM OF ONION SOUP Use only 450 g (1 lb) onions, coat with 25 g (1 oz) flour before frying at stage 3. Add only 900 ml (1½ pt) stock, stir into the onions, bring to the boil, stir until thickened. Proceed as the recipe above. Blend 300 ml (½ pt) single cream into the soup when the onions are tender. Heat gently.

ONION SOUP GRATINÉE Slice Gruyère or other good cooking cheese through the slicing attachment or disc. Put a round of toast or French bread into each heated flameproof soup cup. Pour on the soup and put under a preheated grill for 2 minutes or until the cheese melts.

ONION AND CARROT SOUP Use equal quantities of onions and carrots; slice and cook as the basic recipe. Garnish with chopped parsley.

LEEK AND LEMON SOUP

Serves 4–6
Cooking time 20–25 mins
Use Juice Extractor Attachment of Mixer and Blender *or* Juice Extractor Attachment of Food Processor and Food Processor

450 g (1 lb) leeks
2 tablespoons oil or 25 g (1 oz) butter
900 ml (1½ pt) chicken stock or water and
**　2 chicken stock cubes**
1½–2 lemons
salt and pepper

1　Wash and trim the leeks, chop into pieces. Heat the oil or butter in a saucepan, turn the leeks in this; do not allow to brown.
2　Add the chicken stock, or water and stock cubes.. Cover the pan and simmer for 15–20 minutes or until the leeks are soft; do not over-cook.
3　Spoon the leeks and liquid into the warmed blender goblet; switch on until smooth.
　　Place the double-bladed cutting knife and bowl in position. Spoon the leeks and a little liquid into the bowl, fix the lid and switch on until a smooth purée. Gradually blend in the remaining liquid.
4　Return the purée to the saucepan.
5　Fix the juice extractor; halve the lemons and extract the juice. Add enough juice to the soup to give a strong lemon taste. Season with salt and pepper. Heat the soup or serve cold.

To freeze
This soup is best freshly made.

Fruit soups

Although these soups are very popular in many countries they are not served often in Britain. Try the suggestions on this page. Fruit soups make a particularly good meal starter in hot weather, or when the main course is rather rich or substantial.

A small amount of dried fruits such as diced prunes, raisins or sultanas may be added to any of the following fruit soups. Cook with the fruit and blend at stage 3, or add to the puréed soup.

Based on Avocado Soup

All these mixtures are put into the blender or food processor and made into a smooth purée to serve hot or cold.

APPLE SOUP Use 450 g (1 lb) cooked apples instead of avocados; add a little, but not too much, sugar. Use dry cider in place of stock. Flavour the soup with a pinch grated nutmeg, ground cinnamon and ground ginger. Add soured cream in place of fresh cream.

CARROT AND ORANGE SOUP Use 350 g (12 oz) cooked carrots instead of avocados. Add 300 ml ($\frac{1}{2}$ pt) carrot or chicken stock and 300 ml ($\frac{1}{2}$ pt) canned or fresh orange juice and enough parsley to give 2 tablespoons when chopped.

CARROT AND TOMATO SOUP Use 350 g (12 oz) cooked carrots instead of avocados. Add 150 ml ($\frac{1}{4}$ pt) chicken stock and 450 ml ($\frac{3}{4}$ pt) bottled, canned or freshly prepared tomato juice.

RHUBARB SOUP Use 450 g (1 lb) canned or cooked rhubarb instead of avocados, add a little, but not too much, sugar. Use 150 ml ($\frac{1}{4}$ pt) orange juice, 450 ml ($\frac{3}{4}$ pt) dry white wine instead of chicken stock and cream. Flavour the purée with grated nutmeg. Serve topped with a little natural yogurt or soured cream.

Note Any of the purées prepared above may be made a little thinner with the addition of stock.

AVOCADO SOUP

Serves 4–6
No cooking
Use Juice Extractor Attachment of Mixer and Blender *or* Juice Extractor Attachment of Food Processor and Food Processor

1 lemon
enough chives to give 3 tablespoons when chopped
2 large ripe avocados
450 ml ($\frac{3}{4}$ pt) chicken stock
150 ml ($\frac{1}{4}$ pt) double or single cream

1 Fix the juice extractor, halve the lemon and extract the juice; or use a hand squeezer. Put the juice into a small bowl.
2 Chop the chives in the blender goblet or bowl of the food processor, using the double-bladed cutting knife. Remove about half the chives, leave the rest of the chives in the goblet or food processor bowl.
3 Pour the lemon juice into the blender goblet or bowl of the food processor. Halve and skin the avocados, remove the stones. Chop the pulp roughly and put into the blender goblet or bowl of the food processor; switch on and blend or process. Do this as soon as possible after halving and skinning the avocados so there is no possibility of the fruit discolouring.
4 Add the rest of the ingredients and continue blending or processing.
5 Chill the soup and serve sprinkled with the remaining chives.

To freeze
This soup freezes well for a short time; use within 1 month.

To vary
Use a little white wine in place of some of the stock.
    Serve the soup hot instead of cold.

Note Always use ripe avocados for this soup; under-ripe avocados lack flavour.

Speedy vegetable soups

CARROT SOUP Peel 300 g (10 oz) carrots and 1–2 onions. Put through the grating (shredding) attachment of the mixer or grating disc of the food processor. Heat 50 g (2 oz) butter in a saucepan, add the vegetables and toss. Stir in 900 ml (1½ pt) chicken stock. Bring to the boil and add 1 bay leaf, 1 bouquet garni, 1 tablespoon long-grain rice, 1 teaspoon sugar, salt and pepper to taste. Cook for 15 minutes, or until the rice and vegetables are tender. Serves 4

CRÉCY SOUP Make the cooked rice and vegetable mixture above into a smooth purée in the blender or food processor.

CHESTNUT SOUP De-rind 2–3 bacon rashers, peel 1 onion and 1–2 garlic cloves; chop roughly. Heat 50 g (2 oz) butter in a saucepan, add the bacon, onion and garlic and cook gently for 5 minutes. Add 900 ml (1½ pt) chicken stock and 200 – 225 g (7–8 oz) canned, unsweetened chestnut purée, salt and pepper to taste. Simmer for 15 minutes. Blend or process until smooth.

   Serve with croûtons of fried bread. Serves 4

CHESTNUT AND TOMATO SOUP Follow the recipe above but use tomato juice instead of chicken stock.

COUNTRY TOMATO SOUP

Serves 4–6
Cooking time 10 mins
Use Blender *or* Food Processor

450 g (1 lb) tomatoes
1 medium onion
1–2 rashers streaky bacon
1 small sprig basil
enough parsley to give 2 tablespoons
   when chopped
600 ml (1 pt) chicken stock or water and
   1 chicken stock cube
salt and pepper

1   Halve or quarter the tomatoes. Peel and roughly chop the onion, de-rind and chop the bacon.
B 2   Put all the ingredients into the blender goblet, switch on until smooth. Transfer to a saucepan.
FP   Place the double-bladed cutting knife and bowl in position. Add the tomatoes, onion, bacon, herbs, 2–3 tablespoons stock or water and a little salt and pepper into the bowl. Fix the lid and switch on until a purée. Transfer to the saucepan, add the rest of the stock, or water and stock cube.
3   Simmer for 10 minutes and serve.

To freeze
This soup freezes well for 3 months.

To vary
The onion and bacon can be roughly chopped then fried in a little butter or margarine before adding the rest of the ingredients and cooking, as above. When cooked, put into the blender or food processor and purée.

   As explained on page 10 some particles of tomato skin and some pips may still be left in the purée. For a perfectly smooth soup the mixture must be put through a nylon sieve or the sieve and colander attachment of a mixer, used as described on page 15. You can, of course, skin the tomatoes and remove all pips before making the soup.

CREAM OF TOMATO SOUP Prepare the tomato mixture as the recipe above but use only 450 ml (¾ pt) stock. While the tomato mixture is cooking, make a sauce with 25 g (1 oz) butter or margarine, 25 g (1 oz) flour, 300 ml (½ pt) milk, salt and pepper to taste; see page 70.
B Put the very hot tomato mixture into the heated blender goblet, switch on until a smooth purée.
FP Put the solid ingredients into the bowl, switch on until a smooth purée, mix in the remaining very hot liquid.

   Add the hot white sauce (made as above), blend or process with the tomato mixture without reheating. You then avoid the possibility of the soup curdling, as it might do if the acid tomato mixture is heated with the milky sauce.

An excellent fish starter to serve when entertaining Smoked Haddock Mousse (page 23)

POTAGE ST. GERMAIN

Serves 6
Cooking time 50–55 mins
Use Slicing Attachment of Mixer and
Blender *or* Slicing Disc of Food Processor
and Food Processor

1–2 medium onions
25 g (1 oz) butter or margarine
900 ml (1½ pt) ham stock
350 g (12 oz) shelled or frozen peas
salt and pepper
6–8 peppercorns (optional)
1 small bunch of mint
150 ml (¼ pt) milk
15 g (½ oz) flour
4 tablespoons single or double cream
To garnish
sprigs parsley, fried croûtons of bread

(MA) 1 Peel the onions and put through the
slicing attachment.

[FP] Peel the onions. Place the double-
bladed cutting knife or slicing disc and
bowl in position. Add the onions, fix the
lid and switch on until chopped; or put
through the slicing disc.

2 Melt the butter or margarine in a pan,
add the onions and toss. Add the ham
stock and peas, season well.

3 This soup should have plenty of pepper
so peppercorns as well as a shake of
pepper can be included.

4 Add the mint. Cover the pan and
simmer gently for 25 minutes; remove
the peppercorns and mint.

(B) 5 Put the soup into the warmed goblet
and switch on until a smooth purée;
return to the saucepan.

[FP] Place the double-bladed cutting knife
and bowl in position. Spoon the solid
ingredients into the bowl with a little
liquid, fix the lid and switch on until
smooth; mix with the liquid in the pan.

6 Blend the milk with the flour.

7 Stir into the soup, bring the mixture
slowly to the boil and cook until
thickened, stirring all the time.

(B) 8 Wash and dry the blender or food
(OR)
[FP] processor; chop the parsley in the
blender goblet or bowl of the food
processor, using the double-bladed
cutting knife.

9 Add the cream just before serving.
Garnish with parsley and croûtons.

To freeze
This soup freezes well for 3 months. Add
the cream when reheating.

WATERCRESS SOUP

Serves 4–6
Cooking time 12 mins
Use Blender *or* Food Processor

approximately 100 g (4 oz) watercress
50 g (2 oz) butter, margarine or chicken
fat
50 g (2 oz) flour
450 ml (¾ pt) milk
300 ml (½ pt) chicken stock
salt and pepper
1–2 tablespoons lemon juice
4 tablespoons double cream

1 Wash the watercress and pull off all the
leaves.

2 Heat the butter, margarine or chicken
fat in a saucepan.

3 Stir in the flour and cook over a low heat
for 2 minutes, stirring well.

4 Gradually blend in the milk and stock.
Bring to the boil and continue stirring
over the heat until the sauce has
thickened; add a little salt and pepper.

(B) 5 Pour the sauce into the warmed blender
goblet, add the lemon juice to taste and
the cream, switch on for a few seconds
until a smooth sauce. Remove the lid
and add the watercress leaves. Replace
the lid, switch on again until the
watercress is slightly chopped.

[FP] Place the double-bladed cutting knife
and bowl in position. Add the sauce,
lemon juice and cream, fix the lid and
switch on for a few seconds. Drop the
watercress leaves through the feed-tube
with the machine in operation; process
for 1–2 seconds only.

6 Reheat if necessary but *do not* allow the
sauce to curdle.

To freeze
This soup freezes reasonably well; although
it may become thinner and need a little
extra flour or cornflour when reheating, see
note on page 26. Do not boil when reheating.

To vary
Many cooked vegetables from artichokes,
asparagus, carrots to mixed left-over
vegetables could be blended with the
sauce.

SORREL SOUP Cook 225 g (8 oz) sorrel
with 1–2 chopped leeks in 300 ml (½ pt) well
seasoned water or chicken stock until
tender. Add to the sauce at stage 5 and
blend or process until mixed with the
sauce.

SPINACH SOUP Cook 225–300 g (8-10 oz) young spinach until tender, using the water adhering to the leaves after washing these; do not use extra liquid if possible. Add to the sauce at stage 5 and blend or process until mixed with the sauce.

VELOUTÉ OF WATERCRESS Use 2 egg yolks with the lemon juice and cream. Reheat the soup at stage 6; do not allow to boil.
Note Creamy soups, as above, are improved in texture after a short period of blending or processing.

To make croûtons
Cut slices of bread into small dice. Deep or shallow fry until golden. To freeze, cool, open freeze, then store in polythene bags.

MUSHROOM SOUP

Serves 4–6
Cooking time 15 mins
Use Blender *or* Food Processor

175 g (6 oz) mushrooms*
50 g (2 oz) butter or margarine
25 g (1 oz) flour
**900 ml (1½ pt) chicken stock or water and
    2 chicken stock cubes**
salt and pepper
To garnish
chopped parsley
*Small white button mushrooms produce a better colour but larger field mushrooms give a stronger and better flavour.

1 Wipe or wash the mushrooms, dry well; there is no need to peel good quality mushrooms.
2 Heat the butter or margarine in a saucepan, add the mushrooms and fry steadily for 3–4 minutes. Blend in the flour.
3 Stir in the stock, or water and stock cubes. Bring to the boil, lower the heat and cover the pan. Simmer gently for 6–7 minutes, add salt and pepper to taste.
B 4 Spoon the mushrooms and liquid into the warmed blender goblet; switch on until a smooth purée. Return to the saucepan or serve at once if the purée is sufficiently hot. Garnish with parsley.
FP   Place the double-bladed cutting knife and bowl in position. Lift the mushrooms out of the liquid with a perforated spoon

or fish slice and put into the bowl. Add a few tablespoons liquid from the saucepan, fix the lid and switch on until the mushrooms form a smooth purée. Tip the purée into the saucepan, stir into the mushroom liquid or gradually blend the mushroom liquid into the mushroom purée in the food processor. Reheat the soup for 1 minute. Garnish with parsley and serve.

To freeze
This soup freezes well for up to 6 months.

To vary
Chop 1 peeled onion in the blender or food processor and add to the mushrooms at stage 2.

BEEF AND MUSHROOM SOUP Add about 100 g (4 oz) diced cooked lean beef to the mushrooms at stage 4.

CREAM OF MUSHROOM SOUP Use only 600 ml (1 pt) stock or water with 1-1½ chicken stock cubes and 300 ml (½ pt) milk; proceed as the basic recipe. Stir a few tablespoons double or single cream into the soup just before serving.

CHICKEN AND MUSHROOM SOUP There are two ways of making this soup.
a) Dice about 175 g (6 oz) raw breast of chicken and heat in the butter or margarine at stage 2 before frying the mushrooms (you may need to add a little extra butter or margarine). Continue as the basic recipe, cooking the chicken and mushrooms until tender.
b) Add cooked pieces of chicken to the mushrooms at stage 4. It is a splendid way of using up the last pieces of chicken from the carcass.
    Cooked turkey or game bird flesh could be used instead of chicken.

VELOUTÉ OF MUSHROOMS Prepare the basic mushroom soup as stages 1–3. Make the purée as stage 4 and keep this or the last batch in the blender goblet or bowl of the food processor. Mix 2 egg yolks, 5 tablespoons double cream and 1 tablespoon lemon juice in a bowl. Pour this mixture into the blender or food processor, preferably through the cap in the blender lid (or foil funnel) or feed-tube of the processor with the motor running. This prevents any possibility of the soup curdling. Pour back into the saucepan and simmer, *without boiling*, for several minutes. Whisk or stir during this process.

SLICED MUSHROOM AND ONION SOUP

Slice the raw mushrooms before cooking them in the butter or margarine. Using the slicing attachment of the mixer or slicing disc of the food processor, push the mushrooms through, then continue as stages 2 and 3 of the basic recipe. Additional interest and flavour can be given by slicing 1 or 2 peeled onions with the mushrooms and by substituting beef stock, or water and beef stock cubes, for chicken stock or cubes.

Based upon Mushroom Soup

CHICORY SOUP Use 2–3 heads of white chicory instead of the mushrooms. Chop coarsely and continue as stages 2–4. Add a little lemon juice when simmering the chicory and cook for 5 minutes only.

PEPPER SOUP Use 2 green or red peppers in place of the mushrooms. Chop the flesh coarsely, discard the core and seeds. Continue as stages 2–4. This soup is improved by adding 1–2 chopped leeks to the peppers; use the white part and only a very little green of the leek. Flavour with garlic salt.

SPEEDY ASPARAGUS SOUP

Serves 4–6
No cooking
Use Blender *or* Food Processor

450 g (1 lb) canned asparagus spears
approximately 600 ml (20 fl oz) natural
**   yogurt**
salt and pepper

B OR **FP**   1   Open the can of spears, put nearly all the asparagus and liquid from the can into the blender goblet or bowl of the food processor, using the double-bladed cutting knife, but cut off 4–6 asparagus tips for garnish.

B OR **FP**   2   Switch on for a few seconds, then add the yogurt and continue blending or processing until the mixture is quite smooth. Add salt and pepper to taste.

3   Serve well chilled, topped with the asparagus tips.

To freeze
This soup is better freshly prepared.

To vary
Use half yogurt and half chicken stock or milk, or all milk.

Use cooked fresh asparagus instead of canned.

Serve as a hot soup. If using yogurt, do not allow to boil. To avoid a curdled soup, heat the yogurt separately from the asparagus, then blend the two hot ingredients in the blender or food processor. Serve at once.

Based upon Speedy Asparagus Soup

SPEEDY ARTICHOKE SOUP Use canned or cooked fresh artichoke hearts (often called 'bottoms') instead of asparagus. This soup is improved if 1 peeled clove garlic or a little garlic salt, plus a little double cream, is blended or processed with the other ingredients.

BEETROOT YOGURT SOUP Use canned or cooked and peeled fresh beetroot instead of asparagus. A few spring onions, a small sprig of parsley and a little chives may be blended or processed with the other ingredients.

SPEEDY CHICKEN SOUP Use 350 g (12 oz) cooked chicken breast instead of asparagus. Include also a sprig of parsley, 2 spring onions and a small piece of peeled cucumber.

SPEEDY SPINACH SOUP Use canned or cooked spinach instead of asparagus. A grating of nutmeg and a pinch garlic salt give extra flavour.

Three colourful soups made quickly and easily in a blender or food processor
Bacon and Spinach Soup (page 38).
Mediterranean Fish Soup (page 42).
Creamed Stilton and Onion Soup (page 27).

Meat and poultry soups

Never waste the tiny pieces of flesh and skin on meat or poultry bones. These can be turned into excellent thick purée soups, which can be varied by the addition of various vegetables and herbs. Try the 'Penny-Wise' Chicken Soup, opposite.

Speedy meat and poultry soups

BEEF AND CELERY SOUP Open a large can of celery hearts and cut the celery into smaller pieces. Put into the blender goblet or bowl of the food processor, using the double-bladed cutting knife. Add 225 g (8 oz) diced, good quality cooked beef, a 225 g (8 oz) can of tomatoes and the liquid from both cans. Blend or process until a smooth purée. Dilute with enough beef stock to give the desired consistency. Heat, add garlic salt and pepper to taste. Top with croûtons of fried bread.
Serves 4–6

CHICKEN AND ALMOND SOUP Dice 225–350 g (8–12 oz) cooked breast of chicken and put into the blender goblet or bowl of the food processor, using the double-bladed cutting knife. Add 150 ml ($\frac{1}{4}$ pt) chicken stock and 150 ml ($\frac{1}{4}$ pt) single cream to the blender but do not add all the liquid when using a food processor; add this later. Add a little rosemary, 25 g (1 oz) ground almonds, salt and pepper to taste. Switch on until a smooth purée. With the motor in operation, drop 25–50 g (1–2 oz) blanched almonds through the hole in the lid as page 10 or feed-tube, blend or process for a few seconds only. Tip into a saucepan; dilute the soup with another 300–450 ml ($\frac{1}{2}$–$\frac{3}{4}$ pt) chicken stock and heat.
Serves 4–6

CURRIED CHICKEN SOUP Peel 2 onions and 1 dessert apple, put through the slicing attachment of the mixer or slicing disc of the food processor. Heat 50 g (2 oz) butter in a saucepan and fry the onions and apple until tender. Stir in 25 g (1 oz) flour and 1–2 tablespoons curry powder, cook gently for 2–3 minutes. Add 600 ml (1 pt) chicken stock and 150 ml ($\frac{1}{4}$ pt) single cream,

stirring until smooth and boiling. Add 225–350 g (8–12 oz) minced or diced cooked chicken; heat thoroughly.
Serves 4–6

BACON AND SPINACH SOUP

(Illustrated on page 37)

Serves 4–6
Cooking time 30 mins
Use Blender *or* Food Processor

1 large onion
175 g (6 oz) streaky bacon
50 g (2 oz) butter
450 g (1 lb) frozen leaf or chopped spinach, or fresh spinach
25 g (1 oz) flour
450 ml ($\frac{3}{4}$ pt) milk
450 ml ($\frac{3}{4}$ pt) chicken stock
1–2 tablespoons Worcestershire sauce
salt and pepper
150 ml ($\frac{1}{4}$ pt) single cream

1 Peel the onion and de-rind the bacon; chop both roughly by hand. You may prefer to mince these or chop them in a food processor with the chopping knife, but this is not essential – see stage 3.
2 Heat the butter in a large pan and add the onion and bacon. Fry gently for about 5 minutes until soft. Add the spinach and cover the pan. Heat gently until the frozen spinach has thawed or fresh spinach is lightly cooked.
3 Stir in the flour and cook for 1 minute. Gradually add the milk, stock and Worcestershire sauce, stirring constantly. Bring to the boil, add a little salt and pepper and simmer for 20 minutes.
B 4 Tip the soup into the warmed blender goblet, switch on until smooth.
FP Place the double-bladed cutting knife and bowl in position. Spoon the solid ingredients plus a little liquid into the bowl, fix the lid and switch on until a smooth purée. Add the rest of the liquid through the feed-tube.
5 Return the soup to the pan, stir in nearly all the cream. Reheat the soup, but **do not** allow it to boil. Add extra salt and pepper if necessary.
6 Serve with the remaining cream in a swirl on top of the soup.

To freeze
This soup freezes well for up to 6 weeks.
To vary
Use cabbage instead of spinach.

KIDNEY AND PORT WINE SOUP

Serves 4–6
Cooking time 25 mins
Use Mincer Attachment of Mixer *or* Food Processor

6 lamb's kidneys
2 medium onions
50 g (2 oz) butter or margarine
25 g (1 oz) flour
600 ml (1 pt) beef stock
1 wineglass port wine
salt and pepper
1 teaspoon made mustard
pinch ground ginger

1   Skin the kidneys, halve, core and remove any gristle. Peel and quarter the onions.
2   Put the kidneys, then the onions through the coarse plate (screen) of the mincer. Place the double-bladed cutting knife and bowl in position. Add the kidneys and onions, fix the lid and switch on for 3–4 seconds only, or until the meat and onions are chopped into small pieces, not puréed.
3   Heat the butter or margarine in a saucepan, add the kidneys and onions and fry gently until the onions turn pale golden.
4   Stir in the flour and blend over a low heat. Gradually add the stock and port wine, bring to the boil, stirring all the time, and cook until slightly thickened.
5   Add the rest of the ingredients and simmer gently for 12–15 minutes.

To freeze
This soup freezes well, except the port wine tends to lose flavour; it is therefore advisable to add this when reheating the soup.

To vary
Use 350 g (12 oz) ox instead of lamb's kidneys. At stage 5 cook for 1½ hours and use 1·2 litres (2 pt) stock.

CREAMED KIDNEY SOUP Either top the soup with soured cream, or after stage 5 transfer the soup to a warmed blender goblet or bowl of a food processor, switch on until a smooth purée. Return to the saucepan and add a little fresh or soured cream. Reheat the soup gently but do not boil.

Penny-Wise Poultry or Game Soups

1   Never waste the tiny pieces of meat and skin on the carcass of poultry or game birds.
2   Pull these away from the bones.
3   Put the bones into a saucepan or pressure cooker; cover with water. You can add vegetables and herbs as well as salt and pepper to flavour the liquid.
4   Simmer gently for at least 1 hour; or allow a minimum of 30 minutes at H/15 lb pressure. Strain the stock or use the stock and vegetables; check all bones are discarded.
5   Put the flesh and skin of the bird into the warmed blender goblet or bowl of the food processor. Add enough stock to cover and the vegetables if liked; switch on until a smooth purée.
6   If using rather fat poultry such as duck or goose, it is advisable to prepare the soup ahead, cool, remove surplus fat and reheat.

To freeze
If freezing make a thicker purée that can be diluted and varied at different times. Use within 3 months.

To vary
CHICKEN AND ROSEMARY SOUP Use about 300 g (10 oz) cooked chicken meat and skin, with enough fresh rosemary to give about 2 teaspoons when chopped. Peel 2–3 medium carrots, 1 medium potato and 1 large onion. Cook the vegetables in the liquid when making stock from the carcass. Blend or process the chicken, rosemary, cooked carrots, potato and onion with approximately 750 ml (1¼ pt) stock and 150 ml (¼ pt) single cream. Season well.

DUCK AND ORANGE SOUP Use about 225 g (8 oz) cooked duck meat, plus the finely grated rind and juice of 1–2 oranges. When preparing the stock from the duck carcass, add 2 peeled onions plus several fresh sage leaves. Blend or process the duck, orange rind and juice, cooked onions and sage leaves with approximately 900 ml (1½ pt) stock, season well and add a pinch of brown sugar.
    Goose could be used instead.

Fish soups

Whether you want a soup that is smooth and velvety in texture, or one that contains small pieces of firm fish and vegetables, you will find the various attachments to the mixer, or a food processor, are invaluable.

Do not overcook the fish for this food loses texture and, therefore, flavour very easily.

SALMON AND CUCUMBER SOUP

Serves 6
Cooking time about 15 mins
Use Grating (Shredding) Attachment of Mixer or Grating (Shredding) Disc of Food Processor

½ large cucumber
1 small onion
225 g (8 oz) cooked or canned salmon
25 g (1 oz) butter
25 g (1 oz) flour
600 ml (1 pt) chicken stock or water and
  1 chicken stock cube
1 sprig parsley
salt and pepper
½–1 tablespoon lemon juice
150 ml (¼ pt) natural yogurt or soured
  cream
To garnish
little chopped fennel leaves and/or
  chopped parsley

1 Peel the cucumber and onion.
2 Put the vegetables through the grating (shredding) attachment of the mixer.
   Put the vegetables through the grating disc of the food processor.
3 Flake the salmon, discarding any bones or skin.
4 Melt the butter in a saucepan and fry the onion for several minutes. Stir in the flour and cook gently for 2–3 minutes. Gradually blend in the stock or water and stock cube, together with the sprig of parsley.
5 Bring to the boil and stir over the heat until the mixture thickens slightly.
6 Add the salt and pepper, cucumber and lemon juice, and simmer for 4–5 minutes.
7 Stir in the yogurt or soured cream and the salmon, heat for 2–3 minutes; DO NOT allow the soup to boil.
8 Garnish with the herbs and serve.

To freeze
This soup freezes well, but the cucumber tends to lose its texture. Use within 2 months.

To vary
COLD SALMON AND CUCUMBER SOUP
Omit the flour; use only 450 ml (¾ pt) stock or water; proceed to the end of stage 5. The mixture will not thicken in the same way. Allow to cool, then add the rest of the ingredients as stages 6 and 7, but do not heat the mixture. Garnish and serve.

WHITE FISH SOUP Use cooked white fish and fish stock instead of salmon and chicken stock. Add either 1 teaspoon concentrated tomato purée or anchovy essence to give colour and flavour to the soup.

PURÉED SOUP Make the basic soup or the variation above; put into the blender goblet or bowl of the food processor and switch on until a smooth purée. Serve hot or cold. Garnish with a little extra sliced cucumber and lemon slices.

Speedy fish soups
SALMON AND YOGURT SOUP Put 225 g (8 oz) cooked or canned salmon, 2 or 3 small spring onions, a sprig of parsley and fresh dill, 600 ml (1 pt/20 fl oz) natural yogurt, salt and pepper to taste into the blender goblet or bowl of the food processor. Switch on until a purée. Serve well chilled.
Serves 4

TUNA AND TOMATO SOUP De-rind and chop 2 bacon rashers; fry for 2–3 minutes. Add 600 ml (1 pt) chicken stock, 225 g (8 oz) canned tuna, 3 large, skinned, diced tomatoes, a sprig of parsley, a few fennel leaves, salt and pepper to taste. Place in the blender goblet or bowl of the food processor and switch on until a smooth purée. Heat or serve cold.
Serves 4

Fish can be prepared and cooked in many ways from a thick soup to a main dish with a difference
Finnan Chowder (page 42), Plaice Victoria (page 47)

MEDITERRANEAN FISH SOUP

(Illustrated on page 37)

Serves 4–6
Cooking time 30 mins
Use Juice Extractor and Slicing
Attachments of Mixer *or* Juice Extractor
Attachment and Slicing Disc of Food
Processor

1 lemon
2 medium onions
2 cloves garlic
2 tablespoons oil
2 x 396 g (14 oz) cans tomatoes
1–2 tablespoons Worcestershire sauce
600 ml (1 pt) tomato juice
300 ml (½ pt) water
1 bay leaf
salt and pepper
350 g (12 oz) white fish (weight when
  boned and skinned)
100 g (4 oz) peeled prawns

1   Fix the juice extractor attachment, halve
    the lemon and extract the juice; or use a
    hand squeezer.
2   Peel the onions and garlic; crush the
    garlic by hand or put through the slicer
    at stage 3.
3   Change the juice extractor attachment,
    fix the slicing attachment to the mixer or
    slicing disc to the food processor.
4   Put the onions (and garlic if liked)
    through the slicing attachment or disc.
5   Heat the oil in a large saucepan and
    add the onion and garlic. Fry gently for
    about 5 minutes until soft.
6   Add the canned tomatoes with the
    liquid from the cans, lemon juice,
    Worcestershire sauce, tomato juice,
    water, bay leaf, salt and pepper to taste.
    Bring to the boil and simmer for 15
    minutes.
7   Cut the fish into cubes and add to the
    soup. Simmer for 5 minutes, then add
    the prawns. Continue to simmer for a
    further 5 minutes.
8   Remove the bay leaf, add extra salt and
    pepper if necessary.

To freeze
This soup freezes well for 1 month.

FINNAN CHOWDER

(Illustrated on page 41)

Serves 6–8
Cooking time 25 mins
Use Slicing Attachment of Mixer *or* Slicing
Disc of Food Processor

3 rashers bacon, preferably unsmoked
  (green)
450 ml (¾ pt) water
2 medium onions
350–450 g (12 oz–1 lb) potatoes
salt and pepper
450 g (1 lb) smoked haddock fillet
450 ml (¾ pt) milk
bouquet garni
150 ml (¼ pt) single cream

1   De-rind the bacon and cut the rashers
    into matchstick pieces with kitchen
    scissors. Put the bacon and rinds into a
    saucepan and fry for a few minutes;
    remove the rinds. Add the water and
    bring to the boil.
2   Fix the slicing attachment to the mixer
    or slicing disc to the food processor. If
    your model provides a choice then
    select the one that gives thin slices.
    Peel the onions and potatoes, cut into
    convenient sized pieces to fit into the
    attachment or feed-tube of the food
    processor; press through with the
    pusher.
3   Add the sliced vegetables, a little salt
    and pepper to the bacon and water.
    Simmer for 8 minutes.
4   Meanwhile put the haddock, milk and
    bouquet garni into a second pan, poach
    for 8–10 minutes or until the fish is *just*
    tender. Flake the fish using a fork, and
    discard the bouquet garni.
5   Add the fish, milk and cream to the
    vegetables and bacon. Simmer for 5
    minutes and add extra salt and pepper
    if necessary.

To freeze
This soup is better served freshly made.

To vary
This satisfying soup can be varied by the
addition of other vegetables.

CHAPTER 5

FISH DISHES

Many fish dishes depend upon vegetables and herbs for flavouring, so the comments regarding the preparation of vegetables and herbs on pages 79 to 81 will be helpful. Some fish dishes such as quenelles, moulds or loaves, are made with a smooth purée of raw fish.

Fish using the mincer attachment

Remove any skin and all bones from the fish. In most cases you will find it easier to use the coarser plate (screen) on the mincer first, then afterwards put the minced fish through the finer plate (screen) if the mixture needs to be really smooth. Cut the raw fish into strips about 2.5 cm (1 in) in width. Switch the mixer to medium speed and then feed the fish through, pressing it down with the pusher. Herbs may be minced with the fish.

Fish using the food processor

Raw fish is chopped very successfully with the double-bladed cutting knife. Remove any skin and all bones; cut the fish into 3.5–5-cm ($1\frac{1}{2}$–2-in) pieces. Place the double-bladed cutting knife and bowl in position. Add the fish in 225 g (8 oz) batches, fix the lid and switch on for about 5 seconds only. Remove the lid, check on the fineness of the fish, process for a further 2–3 seconds if necessary. Do not over-process, otherwise the fish becomes slightly over-sticky.

Herbs may be chopped with the fish and a little salt and pepper added before processing. Do not over-season as processing is inclined to intensify seasoning.

STUFFED PLAICE

Serves 4
Cooking time 30–35 mins
Use Slicing Attachment of Mixer *or* Slicing
Disc of Food Processor

2 large plaice
1 medium onion
50 g (2 oz) mushrooms
1 lettuce
75 g (3 oz) butter
little lemon juice
salt and pepper
To garnish
6 lemon slices, few sprigs parsley

1 Cut the plaice into 8 fillets or ask the fishmonger to do this.

(MA) OR (FP) 2 Peel the onion, wash and dry the mushrooms, and wash the lettuce. Put through the slicing attachment of the mixer or slicing disc of the food processor.

3 Heat 50 g (2 oz) butter in a pan, add the vegetables with a little lemon juice, salt and pepper and cook gently until tender.

4 Put half the fish fillets into an ovenproof dish, cover with the lettuce stuffing, remaining fillets and a little salt and pepper.

5 Melt the remaining butter and pour over the fish. Cover the dish and cook in the centre of a moderately hot oven, 200°C, 400°F, Gas Mark 6, for 20–25 minutes. Top with the lemon slices and sprigs of parsley.

To freeze
Cooked fish loses flavour and texture. It is therefore better to prepare the dish, freeze for up to 3 months, then defrost and cook.

To vary
STUFFED TROUT The lettuce stuffing above is excellent for fresh trout. Remove the heads and split 4 fish, then cut away the backbones. Fill with the stuffing, then proceed as the recipe above.

FISH QUENELLES

Serves 6 as an hors d'oeuvre or 4 as a main course
Cooking time 20 mins (plus making stock)
Use Mincer Attachment of Mixer *or* Food Processor

450 g (1 lb) white fish* (weight without bones or skin)
For the panada
25 g (1 oz) butter or margarine
25 g (1 oz) flour
150 ml (¼ pt) milk or single cream
salt and pepper
2 egg yolks
enough fennel, parsley or tarragon to give 1 tablespoon when chopped
To poach
600 ml (1 pt) fish stock (see page 46)
To serve
melted butter or sauce (see below)

*The traditional fish for Quenelles is pike. This is often difficult to obtain so use whiting, sole or plaice. If using a food processor, you can select larger flaked fish as the mixture is made exceptionally smooth. The food processor produces the same texture as the old fashioned pestle and mortar.

(MA) 1 Mince the raw fish, see page 43. It is advisable to mince twice to give a fine texture.

(FP)   Dice and process the fish, see page 43. Leave the fish in the bowl.

2 Make a panada (thick coating sauce). Heat the butter or margarine, stir in the flour and cook for 2 minutes, over a low heat. Blend in the milk or cream. Bring to the boil, stirring, and cook until thickened. Add salt, pepper and the egg yolks.

(MA) 3 Mix the sauce with the minced fish, pounding well. Mince the herbs and add to the fish mixture.

(FP)   Add the sauce to the processed fish. Fix the lid and switch on for 2–3 seconds, drop the herbs through the feed-tube and continue processing until finely chopped.

4 Allow to cool, form into finger shapes or use spoonfuls of the mixture.

5 Heat the stock in a large frying pan and poach the Quenelles for 10 minutes, turning them gently so they are cooked evenly.

6 Drain and top with melted butter or serve with a sauce, e.g. Hollandaise, Tartare or Herb Sauce, pages 71, 73, 70.

To freeze
The uncooked Quenelle mixture can be frozen for up to 6 weeks. Defrost and continue from stage 4.

To vary
FISH CREAM Use 200 ml (⅓ pt/7½ fl oz) milk or single cream instead of 150 ml (¼ pt) to make a thinner sauce. Put the Quenelle mixture into a greased mould and steam over hot, but not boiling, water for 1 hour. Serve with one of the sauces suggested above.

CHICKEN OR TURKEY QUENELLES Use chicken or turkey breast and chicken or turkey stock instead of fish and fish stock.

GAME QUENELLES Use tender pheasant or grouse breast and game stock instead of fish and fish stock.

More dishes with cut raw fish

In each case mince or process 450 g (1 lb) white fish (weight without skin and bone) as page 43. Dishes serve 4.

NORWEGIAN FISH BALLS Blend the fish with 25 g (1 oz) flour, 25 g (1 oz) melted butter, 2 tablespoons single cream, salt, pepper and grated nutmeg to taste. Form into tiny balls, poach gently for 15 minutes in fish stock, see page 46. Serve with melted butter or a sauce, see pages 68–75.

FISH MOULD Blend the fish with 40 g (1½ oz) melted butter, 2 small eggs, 25 g (1 oz) flour, 2 tablespoons single cream, salt and pepper. Put into a greased basin, cover with greased greaseproof paper and foil. Steam for 45 minutes. Serve with one of the sauces on page 70.

Two hearty fish main courses
Fish Cobbler (page 48), Huss Provençal (page 46)

HUSS PROVENCAL

(Illustrated on page 45)

Serves 4–6
Cooking time 50 mins
Use Slicing Attachment of Mixer and Mixer
or Slicing Disc of Food Processor and Food
Processor

675 g (1½ lb) huss or coley fillets
450 ml (¾ pt) fish stock (see below)
1 large onion
1 clove garlic
4 sticks celery
100 g (4 oz) mushrooms
1 tablespoon oil
25 g (1 oz) flour
396 g (14 oz) can tomatoes
pinch dried thyme
1 bay leaf
salt and pepper
1 teaspoon sugar
**675 g (1½ lb) potatoes (weight when
    peeled)**
To garnish
1 large tomato

1 Skin the fish and cut into 2.5-cm (1-in)
   pieces. Put the fish stock into a
   saucepan or deep frying pan, add the
   fish and cover the pan. Poach the fish
   for 5–10 minutes or until tender.
2 Drain the fish and reserve the liquid.
3 Peel the onion and garlic. Wash the
   celery and mushrooms, do not skin
   these.
4 Fix the slicing attachment to the mixer
   or slicing disc to the food processor.
   Press the onion and garlic and then the
   other vegetables through with the
   pusher; keep the onion and garlic
   separate as these are to be fried.
5 Heat the oil in a large saucepan, add
   the onion and garlic and fry for several
   minutes.
6 Stir in the flour and cook over a low heat
   for 2 minutes. Gradually blend in the
   fish stock, bring to the boil and stir until
   the sauce has thickened.
7 Add the sliced celery and mushrooms,
   together with the canned tomatoes and
   liquid from the can, the thyme, bay leaf,
   extra salt and pepper if necessary and
   sugar. Simmer gently, uncovered, for 30
   minutes, during which time the mixture
   will thicken.

8 Meanwhile, peel and cook the potatoes
   in boiling salted water until tender.
   Mash with the whisk(s) or beater of the
   mixer or the double-bladed cutting
   knife of the food processor as described
   on page 81.
9 Put the mashed potatoes into a large
   piping bag, fitted with a 1-cm (½-in)
   potato rose nozzle and pipe into a ring
   on a heated serving dish.
10 Cut the tomato into half, then into wafer-
   thin slices. Remove the pips and pulp
   and add to the tomato mixture in the
   saucepan. Arrange the pieces of tomato
   skin on the creamed potatoes to give
   colour. Put the potato ring into the oven
   to keep hot.
11 Add the diced fish to the tomato mixture
   and heat for 5 minutes, then spoon into
   the centre of the creamed potato ring
   and serve.

To freeze
This dish can be frozen for 2 months.

To make fish stock
Put the bones and skin of fish into a
saucepan, cover with water, add a little salt
and pepper, a bay leaf or bouquet garni.
Cover the pan and simmer for 20–30
minutes. Strain and use.

To freeze
Fish stock freezes well for up to 3 months.

To vary
Add a little celery, onion and/or carrot to
flavour.
   Use half water and half white wine or dry
cider, or add a little lemon juice or white
wine vinegar to the water. Remember if
you use a high percentage of acid wine or
cider or lemon juice in the liquid, there
could be a greater risk of sauces curdling if
cream and/or egg yolks are added at a
later stage.

PLAICE VICTORIA

(Illustrated on page 41)

Serves 4
Cooking time 30 mins
Use Blender and Grating (Shredding)
Attachment of Mixer *or* Food Processor and
Grating (Shredding) Disc of Food Processor

**450 g (1 lb) plaice fillets (weight without
bones)**
300 ml (½ pt) milk
salt and pepper
40 g (1½ oz) butter or margarine
40 g (1½ oz) flour
1 tablespoon capers
**enough parsley to give 1 tablespoon
when chopped**
1 tablespoon lemon juice
**450 g (1 lb) potatoes (weight when
peeled)**
2 tablespoons oil
To garnish
1 lemon, sprigs of parsley

1 Skin the fish and put into a shallow
saucepan or frying pan with the milk
and a little salt and pepper. Poach for
5–8 minutes or until the fish is just
tender.

2 Lift the fish from the milk and flake into
an ovenproof mixing bowl; retain the
milk for the sauce.

3 Heat the butter or margarine in a
saucepan, stir in the flour and cook over
a low heat for 2 minutes. Gradually
blend in the milk, stirring as the sauce
comes to the boil and thickens. As this
sauce is of a binding consistency, it
must be stirred very briskly.

B
OR
FP
4 The easiest way to ensure a perfect
sauce and chop the capers and parsley
at the same time is to either put the
sauce into the warmed blender goblet
or bowl of the food processor, using the
double-bladed cutting knife. Switch on
for a few seconds then drop the capers
and parsley through the hole in the lid
of the blender as described on page 11
or the feed-tube of the food processor
with the machine in operation and leave
on for 2–3 seconds.

5 Tip the sauce into the bowl with the fish
and lemon juice (this could be made by
using the juice extractor attachment)
and blend together. Cover the bowl
with foil and keep hot in the oven.

MA
OR
FP
6 Fix the grating (shredding) attachment
to the mixer or grating (shredding) disc
to the food processor. Peel the potatoes,
cut into convenient sized pieces to fit
into the attachment of the mixer or feed-
tube of the food processor, and press
through with the pusher.

7 Dry the grated potatoes on absorbent
paper.

8 Heat 1 tablespoon of the oil in a 20-cm
(8-in) frying pan; put in half the grated
potatoes, fry steadily for about 5 minutes
or until the potato cake is crisp and
brown. Insert a fish slice under the
potato cake, turn over and cook for the
same time on the second side.

9 Slide the cooked potato cake on to a
heated serving dish and keep hot in the
oven.

10 Heat the remaining oil in the frying pan
and repeat stage 8 with the rest of the
grated potato.

11 Top the first potato cake with the fish
mixture, then cover with the second
potato cake. Cut the lemon into slices,
twist and put on the fish dish, together
with small sprigs of parsley, serve at
once.

To freeze
This dish is not suitable for freezing,
although it is an excellent way of using
frozen fish.

To vary
Grate 1 peeled small onion with the
potatoes at stage 6.
    Use other white fish, such as cod, hake or
fresh haddock.
    Prepare the recipe to the end of stage 5:

FISH PANCAKES Cook 8–12 pancakes as
page 84. Fill with the hot fish mixture.

FISH PASTIES Make shortcrust pastry with
350 g (12 oz) flour, etc. as page 84. Roll out
and cut into 6 rounds. Fill with the fish
mixture. Moisten and seal the pastry to form
pasty shapes. Put on to a baking tray, and
cook in the centre of a moderately hot
oven, 200°C, 400°F, Gas Mark 6 for 25–30
minutes.

FISH COBBLER

(Illustrated on page 45)

Serves 4–6
Cooking time 35–40 mins
Use Slicing and Grating Attachments of
Mixer and Mixer *or* Slicing Disc of Food
Processor and Food Processor

2 medium onions
2 medium carrots
2 sticks celery
100 g (4 oz) button mushrooms
225 g (8 oz) tomatoes
2 tablespoons oil
salt and pepper
1 tablespoon lemon juice
675 g (1½ lb) white fish
For the scone topping
50 g (2 oz) cheese
50 g (2 oz) cooked potato
175 g (6 oz) self-raising flour with 1½
teaspoons baking powder or plain flour
with 3 teaspoons baking powder
salt
40 g (1½ oz) butter
about 6 tablespoons milk
To glaze
1 egg

1 Peel the onions and carrots. Wash the celery and mushrooms. Wipe the tomatoes and slice with a sharp knife.
2 Fit the slicing attachment to the mixer or slicing disc to the food processor. Press the onions, carrots, celery and mushrooms through with the pusher.
3 Heat the oil in a saucepan and fry the onions, carrots, celery, mushrooms and tomatoes for 5–10 minutes until just tender.
4 Season with salt and pepper, and add the lemon juice.
5 Cut the fish into medium-sized chunks.
6 Transfer the vegetables to an ovenproof casserole and add the fish.
7 Fit the grating attachment to the mixer and press the cheese through with the pusher. Put the cooked potato into the

mixer bowl and mash with the whisk(s) or beater; leave in the bowl.

Place the double-bladed cutting knife and bowl in position. Add the cheese, fix the lid and switch on for a few seconds until the cheese is finely chopped. Tip out of the bowl. Add the potatoes to the bowl, fix the lid, switch on again and mash the potatoes; leave in the bowl.

8 Sift the flour, baking powder and pinch of salt into the bowl with the mashed potato. Cut the butter in pieces and add to the flour.

9 Use the whisk(s) or beater, switch to low speed and blend the butter into the flour mixture as described on page 84; add the cheese and enough milk to make a soft, but not sticky, dough.

Fix the lid and switch on for a few seconds until the butter is blended into the flour mixture as described on page 84; add the cheese and then the milk through the feed-tube with the machine in operation; do this steadily until the mixture forms a soft, but not sticky, dough.

10 Turn on to a floured board, knead lightly until smooth.
11 Roll out to about 0·5 cm (¼ in) in thickness, cut out approximately 16 rounds with a 3·5-cm (1½-in) cutter.
12 Cover the surface of the fish and vegetables with overlapping scones.
13 Beat the egg and use to brush over the scones.
14 Bake in the centre of a moderately hot oven, 200°C, 400°F, Gas Mark 6, for 25–30 minutes, reduce the heat slightly after 15 minutes if the scones are becoming too brown.
Serve hot.

To freeze
This dish freezes well for 2 months, although care must be taken that the dish is only lightly cooked at stage 14; for fish loses both taste and texture if it is over-cooked. Thoroughly reheat this dish after defrosting.

CHAPTER 6

MEAT, POULTRY AND GAME DISHES

Although it is easy to buy raw minced beef from a butcher or supermarket it is very difficult to obtain other minced meats, so it is a great advantage to be able to buy the meat and prepare it at home.

Raw minced meat and poultry is an ingredient of a great variety of dishes and a selection of recipes will be found on pages 50 to 63.

Minced meat deteriorates rapidly due to the many cut surfaces; it is therefore an asset to be able to buy portions of meat and chop or mince them just before use.

Left-over cooked meat can be turned into the most tempting savoury dishes.

Meat, poultry and game using the mincer attachment

Most mincer attachments have both a fine and coarser mincing plate (often called a screen). Lean, good quality raw or cooked poultry, game or meat can be put through either plate. You may find it better to put tougher meat through the coarser plate first and then mince it a second time, either through the same plate or the finer one. This will produce soft-textured meat.

Cut the raw meat, poultry or game into strips about 2·5 cm (1 in) in width, making quite sure that there are no bones or pieces of tough gristle that could impede the mincing process. Switch the mixer to medium speed, then feed the meat gradually through the hopper, pressing it down firmly, but not too vigorously, with the pusher. NEVER use your fingers even if the meat seems to be 'jamming' the mincer.

Cooked meat should be minced in the same way. The skin of cooked poultry or game can be minced.

Meat, poultry or game using the food processor

The food processor chops raw meats most successfully, using the double-bladed cutting knife. Remove any excess fat and gristle, then cut the meat into 2·5–3-cm (1–1¼-in) dice; really tender steak or cooked meat can be cut slightly larger, 3·5–5-cm (1½–2-in) dice, particularly when fairly coarsely chopped meat is needed. Process about 225 g (8 oz) meat at one time. Place the double-bladed cutting knife and bowl in position. Add the meat, fix the lid and switch on for about 4–5 seconds only. Remove the lid, check the fineness of the meat; there are many dishes where a fairly coarsely-chopped meat is ideal and this timing should be adequate. If you require the meat to be chopped very finely, allow approximately 7 seconds. It is possible to process the meat, poultry or game until it is a fine purée.

Cooked meat, poultry or game is chopped in the same way. The skin of poultry or game can be included as it becomes very smooth in texture.

Making stews

Many stews contain some sliced vegetables. It saves an appreciable amount of time if you use the slicing attachment of a mixer or slicing disc of a food processor. If you have a choice, select the slicer that produces the thickest slices, for when vegetables are sliced by these appliances they are not only neater than when cut by hand with a knife, but they are generally more thinly sliced. Therefore, you will need to adjust the cooking time if you want them to retain a good texture and flavour. This

49

means adding the vegetables later in the cooking time or frying a few with the meat or poultry, then adding the remainder later. It is a great advantage to have thinly sliced or chopped vegetables when cooking minced meat.

Meat cakes and meat balls

Hamburgers have become extremely popular with both children and adults. The recipes that follow will prove how simple they are to prepare. The golden rule when cooking these, or indeed any meat cakes, is to make quite sure the meat is not over-cooked and dried.

HAMBURGERS

The classic Hamburger is extremely simple to make. It is based on *freshly* prepared meat and should therefore be shaped and cooked as soon as possible after mincing or chopping. Use little salt as this draws out the meat juices too soon.

Serves 4
Cooking time See method
Use Mincer Attachment of Mixer *or* Food Processor

450 g (1 lb) topside of beef, rump or good quality chuck steak
salt and pepper
fat (see method)

1 Dice the meat, mince or process as the directions on page 49. The fine mincer plate (screen) makes the meat easier to shape, but it is better to use the coarser plate if you like underdone Hamburgers. Season with salt and pepper.
2 Form the mixture into 8 cakes about 2 cm (¾ in) in thickness with your fingers or use a Hamburger presser.
3 If the meat has a good proportion of fat do not add extra fat to the frying pan; if very lean meat, use 25 g (1 oz) fat.

4 To fry: preheat the pan, or fat in the pan, and cook for 2–3 minutes on each side, or to personal taste.
To grill: preheat the grill, grease the grid of the grill pan and cook for the same time as for frying. Brush with melted butter or fat when turning the Hamburgers.
To bake: grease and heat a baking tray. Put the Hamburgers on the tray and cook towards the top of a moderately hot to hot oven, 200–220°C, 400–425°F, Gas Mark 6–7, for about 8–10 minutes.
5 Serve the Hamburgers in toasted and buttered rolls, or with vegetables or salad.

To freeze
Open freeze the uncooked Hamburgers, then wrap. Use within 3 months.

To vary
There are many toppings for Hamburgers, e.g. cooked bacon; baked beans; chutney; fried, poached or scrambled eggs; cooked apple or pineapple rings (or other fruit).
Flavour the meat with various chopped fresh or dried herbs, e.g. basil, chives, garlic or parsley.

CHEESEBURGERS Grate or slice cheese as page 64. Place on the cooked Hamburgers and melt in the oven or under the grill.

ECONOMY HAMBURGERS
a) Make 50 g (2 oz) breadcrumbs, see page 28. Add to the meat with 1 egg.
b) Mince or chop 1 peeled medium raw potato and 1 peeled medium onion with the meat. Add chopped parsley to taste.
c) Blend 75–100 g (3–4 oz) mashed potato, see page 81, with the meat; moisten with a little milk or egg if necessary.
d) Add 25 g (1 oz) rolled oats to the meat. Mince or chop 1 peeled medium onion with the meat.

LAMBURGERS Use minced lamb instead of beef. Mince or chop fresh mint and/or rosemary and 1–2 peeled cloves garlic with the meat.

LIVERBURGERS Mince or chop 350 g (12 oz) calf's or lamb's liver and 100 g (4 oz) fat bacon together with 1 peeled medium onion. To give a milder flavour, add 50 g (2 oz) soft breadcrumbs and 1 tablespoon tomato purée. Add a pinch of sugar with the seasoning.

PORKBURGERS Use minced lean pork instead of beef. Mince or chop 1 peeled medium raw potato and 1 peeled medium onion and a few sage leaves with the meat.

VEALBURGERS Mince or chop 300 g (10 oz) lean veal and 175 g (6 oz) bacon or pork together. Flavour as Porkburgers.

FRICADELLES

These Dutch meat balls combine 3 meats to give an interesting blending of flavours.

Serves 6
Cooking time 10 mins
Use Mincer Attachment of Mixer *or* Food Processor

50 g (2 oz) bread (weight without crusts)
milk to cover
1 large onion
225 g (8 oz) lean pork
225 g (8 oz) tender stewing steak or topside
225 g (8 oz) veal
enough parsley to give 1 tablespoon when chopped
salt and pepper
1 egg
pinch ground nutmeg
To coat
25 g (1 oz) flour
To fry
50–75 g (2–3 oz) butter
1 tablespoon oil

1 Put the bread into a bowl, cover with milk and allow to stand for 15 minutes. Strain off the surplus milk. Beat the bread until smooth.
2 Peel and halve the onion. Dice the meats.
   Put the meats, then onion and finally the parsley through the fine plate (screen) of the mincer. Add to the bread.
   Place the double-bladed cutting knife and bowl in position. Add the meats, fix the lid and switch on until the meats are finely chopped. Add to the bread. Process the onion and parsley until finely chopped; add to the meat mixture.
3 Add salt, pepper, egg and nutmeg to the meat mixture and combine well. Form into about 18 small balls with your fingers.
4 Blend the flour with a little salt and pepper. Roll the balls in the seasoned flour.

5 Heat the butter and oil in a frying pan and fry the meat balls steadily for about 8 minutes. Serve with vegetables or a salad.

To freeze
Cook as above or form into balls and open freeze, then pack. Use within 3 months.

To vary
DUTCH KLOPSE Prepare the balls to the end of stage 3. Put 1·2 litres (2 pt) water into a saucepan and add 2 tablespoons cider vinegar. Poach the meat balls for 10 minutes. Meanwhile make a thin sauce with 50 g (2 oz) butter, 25 g (1 oz) flour, 450 ml (¾ pt) beef stock, or water and 1 beef stock cube, season well. Lift the meat balls from the water and vinegar and add to the sauce. Simmer for a further 10 minutes in the sauce. Add 2–3 teaspoons capers to the sauce. Serve with rice.

ITALIAN MEAT BALLS Use the ingredients as the basic recipe, but mince or chop 1–2 peeled cloves garlic with the onion. Fry the meat balls as the basic recipe, leave these in the frying pan but pour off any excess fat. Prepare 450 ml (¾ pt) tomato purée in the blender or food processor. Mince or chop 1 or 2 peeled onions and 1–2 peeled cloves garlic. Add the tomato purée, onions and garlic to the meat balls in the frying pan and simmer for 10–15 minutes. Serve with cooked noodles, spaghetti or rice.

KJØTTKAKER Add 2–3 teaspoons capers and 2 tablespoons double cream to the Fricadelles ingredients. Form this soft mixture into small balls or flat cakes with floured hands. Heat 50 g (2 oz) butter in the frying pan. Fry the meat balls or cakes on each side, then add 450 ml (¾ pt) thin Cheese Sauce, see page 70, to the frying pan, and simmer for 10 minutes.

MEAT BALL KEBABS

The recipe for Fricadelles, or a more savoury meat ball made by adding minced garlic and mixed spice, can be adapted to make Arabic Kebabs. Prepare the meat ball mixture. Oil long metal skewers and mould the meat around them with your fingers. Brush each meat ball with a little well seasoned oil. Cook steadily under a hot grill, turning once or twice. Slices of green or red pepper, small tomatoes and button mushrooms can be cooked with the meat.

MEAT BALLS

Serves 4–6
Cooking time 4 mins
Use Mincer Attachment of Mixer *or* Food
Processor

450 g (1 lb) lamb
1 large onion
salt and pepper
To coat
2 tablespoons flour
1 egg
1 tablespoon water
about 50 g (2 oz) crisp breadcrumbs
To fry
oil or fat

MA 1   Cut the lamb into pieces, put through
the fine plate (screen) of the mincer.
Peel and mince the onion.

FP   Dice the meat. Place the double-bladed
cutting knife and bowl in position. Put
half the meat into the bowl, fix the lid
and switch on for a few seconds until
the meat is finely chopped. Transfer to a
bowl. Repeat with the remaining meat,
and transfer to the bowl. Peel the onion,
cut into quarters and chop very finely in
the processor.

2   Add a little salt and pepper to the
minced lamb and onion. Divide into
about 40 equal sized portions and roll
into balls, pressing the mixture quite
firmly.

3   Mix a little salt and pepper with the
flour, then roll the balls very gently in
the seasoned flour.

4   Beat the egg with the water, brush over
the meat balls, then coat in the crisp
breadcrumbs; make certain the
meat balls are well covered with the
crumbs.

5   Chill for 1 hour if possible; this helps
retain their shape.

6   Heat the oil or fat to 175°C, 347°F, or
until a cube of day-old bread turns
golden within 1 minute. Fry the meat
balls until crisp and brown; drain on
absorbent paper and push a cocktail
stick into each ball. Arrange on a flat
dish with a bowl of Barbecue Sauce, see
opposite.

To freeze
Fry the meat balls, open freeze, then cover.
Use within 3 months.

BARBECUE SAUCE

Serves 4
No cooking
No appliance needed

3 tablespoons tomato ketchup
1½ tablespoons Worcestershire sauce
1½ tablespoons fruit sauce or smooth
   chutney
2–3 teaspoons honey
1 teaspoon French mustard
salt and pepper

Mix all the ingredients together.

VEGETABLE RISOTTO

Serves 4–6
Cooking time 30 mins
Use Slicing Attachment of Mixer *or* Slicing
Disc of Food Processor

2 medium onions
1 aubergine
salt and pepper
1 green pepper
2 tablespoons oil
225 g (8 oz) long grain rice
pinch saffron powder
600 ml (1 pt) chicken stock

1   Peel and quarter the onions. Dice the
unpeeled aubergine, sprinkle with a
little salt and allow to stand for about 30
minutes then pour away the excess
liquid (this draws out the juices from the
skin, which give a bitter flavour). Dice
the pepper, discarding the core and
seeds.

MA
OR
FP 2   Fix the slicing attachment of the mixer
or slicing disc of the food processor and
press the onions through with the
pusher.

3   Heat the oil in a saucepan, add the
vegetables and toss for a few minutes.

4   Add the rice, stir into the oil and
vegetable mixture.

5   Blend the saffron with the stock and
pour over the rice. Bring the liquid to
the boil, stirring briskly, cover the pan
and simmer steadily for 15–20 minutes
or until the rice is tender and the excess
liquid has been absorbed.

Savoury loaves

The recipes following can form the basis for a variety of loaves based upon meat, poultry or game. It is important to keep the mixture moist by using a recipe with a good balance of moisture and to cook the loaf carefully. For Liver Loaf it is recommended in stage 4 that the tin containing the meat mixture is placed in a 'bain-marie' (water bath). This prevents the lean meat mixture from becoming dry and crumbly.

MEAT LOAF

Serves 6–8
Cooking time 1¼–1½ hours
Use Mincer Attachment of Mixer *or* Food Processor

1 large onion
25 g (1 oz) fat
450 g (1 lb) lean beef
225 g (8 oz) veal
225 g (8 oz) pork sausage meat or pork
50 g (2 oz) breadcrumbs
2 eggs
150 ml (¼ pt) beef stock or water and ½
    beef stock cube
1 teaspoon chopped fresh or ½ teaspoon
    dried thyme
1 tablespoon chopped parsley
salt and pepper

1. Peel the onion, put through the coarse plate (screen) of the mincer or chop in the bowl of the food processor, using the double-bladed cutting knife.
2. Heat the fat, add the onion and fry for a few minutes.
3. Dice the beef, veal and pork (if using this rather than pork sausage meat) and mince or chop in the food processor, see information on page 49.
4. Mix the meats with the rest of the ingredients. Grease a large loaf tin and put in the meat mixture. Cover with greased foil and bake in the centre of a moderate oven, 160°C, 325°F, Gas Mark 3, for 1¼–1½ hours.
5. Turn out and serve the meat loaf hot or put a light weight on the loaf and allow to cool.

To freeze
Freeze the loaf in the tin, then turn out and wrap. Use within 3 months.

To vary
CREAMY LOAF Use single cream instead of stock or water and ½ stock cube.

CURRIED LOAF Blend 2 teaspoons curry powder with the fried onion.

LUXURY LOAF Use half red wine and half stock or water, do not add a stock cube.

MEAT AND VEGETABLE LOAF Peel 1 large carrot and 1 medium potato, mince or put through the grating attachment of the mixer or grating disc of the food processor. Thickly slice 50 g (2 oz) mushrooms and dice 1 red pepper, discarding the core and seeds. Mix the vegetables with the meat and cook as the basic recipe.

CHICKEN AND HAM LOAF Use 675 g (1½ lb) raw chicken meat instead of beef and veal. Use a mixture of chicken breast and leg meat. Substitute minced or chopped ham for the pork. The proportions of chicken and ham can be adapted as liked; equal amounts of chicken and ham produce an excellent result. To give a more delicate flavour use single cream instead of stock.

PHEASANT LOAF Use 675 g (1½ lb) raw pheasant instead of beef and veal with the pork sausage meat.

Additions to meat loaves
Never allow a meat loaf to become monotonous by always using exactly the same ingredients. The texture and flavour of the recipes on this page can be changed by adding one or more of the following ingredients to the meat mixture.

a) 2 medium raw carrots. Peel the carrots and mince or finely chop.
b) 3–4 diced gherkins and 1 tablespoon capers.
c) 25–50 g (1–2 oz) sliced, stuffed olives or chopped pickled walnuts.
d) A little soy sauce or Worcestershire sauce, or a few drops of Tabasco sauce.
e) Additional chopped fresh herbs such as chives, rosemary or tarragon.
f) 75–100 g (3–4 oz) sliced raw mushrooms; choose tiny button mushrooms.

Using liver wisely

Liver is an important protein food and also a good source of iron. Unfortunately many people dislike liver. Often, though, they find it more palatable served in a manner given in the loaf on this page.

You can also make liver very attractive if you try these suggestions.

LIVER SOUFFLÉ Mince or chop 225 g (8 oz) raw liver, see Liver Loaf stage 1. Blend with a thick White Sauce, see page 70, using 25 g (1 oz) butter, 25 g (1 oz) flour, 150 ml ($\frac{1}{4}$ pt) milk, 3 egg yolks and 4 stiffly whisked egg whites and salt and pepper to taste. Spoon into a greased soufflé dish and bake in the centre of a moderately hot oven, 190°C, 375°F, Gas Mark 5, for 30 minutes.

LIVER LOAF

Serves 4–6 as a main dish, 8–10 as an hors d'oeuvre
Cooking time 1$\frac{1}{2}$ hours
Use Mincer Attachment of Mixer *or* Food Processor

450 g (1 lb) calf's, lamb's or pig's liver
100 g (4 oz) long streaky bacon
2 medium onions
50 g (2 oz) white or wholemeal bread
   (weight without crusts)
2 eggs
salt and pepper
To line tin
225 g (8 oz) long streaky bacon
To garnish
lettuce, watercress

(MA) 1 Cut the liver into narrow strips and put through the mincer attachment of the mixer using the coarse or fine plate, depending upon personal taste. De-rind the bacon and cut into pieces. Peel and halve the onions. Put them through the mincer together with the bread. Transfer to a mixing bowl and mix in the eggs, salt and pepper to taste.

FP Dice the liver, de-rind and dice the bacon. Peel and cut the onions in quarters. Place the double-bladed cutting knife and bowl in position. Add the liver, bacon and onion, fix the lid and switch on for a few seconds only. Keep the machine running, then drop the bread through the feed-tube; continue processing until all the ingredients are finely chopped. Remove the lid of the processor, add the eggs, salt and pepper to taste. Replace the lid, switch on for a few seconds only.

2 De-rind the remaining bacon and line the base and sides of a 1-kg (2-lb) loaf tin with most of the rashers; save 3 rashers for the top.

3 Spoon in the liver mixture. Halve the 3 bacon rashers and place over the liver mixture.

4 Stand the tin in another dish or tin of cold water (a bain-marie); this keeps the sides of the mixture moist during cooking.

5 Bake in the centre of a moderate oven, 160°C, 325°F, Gas Mark 3, for 1$\frac{1}{2}$ hours. Turn out of the tin on to a heated serving dish if serving hot. Garnish with lettuce and watercress.

6 Serve hot with a Tomato or Brown Sauce, see pages 75 and 68. To serve cold, leave in the tin and place a thick piece of greaseproof paper and a light weight over the top of the loaf and allow to become quite cold. Garnish and serve with a salad.

To freeze
This loaf freezes well for up to 3 months.

To vary
PIQUANT LIVER LOAF Mix 2 finely chopped tomatoes, 1 tablespoon tomato purée and 1 teaspoon Worcestershire sauce into the other ingredients.

FP If using a food processor quarter the tomatoes, add to the liver mixture, together with the above ingredients, before adding the eggs. Cook as above.

BEEF LOAF Use raw topside of beef or best quality chuck steak instead of liver. Cook as above.

CHICKEN LOAF Use raw chicken meat (a mixture of breast and leg meat gives the best flavour) instead of liver. Cook for 1$\frac{1}{4}$ hours only.

A touch of luxury
Prime quality meat can be minced and served as a luxury dish. One of the most famous luxury meat dishes is Steak Tartare.

The method of cooking minced liver in a savoury custard is less well-known but it is an admirable dish for anyone on a light diet.

STEAK TARTARE

This dish is best prepared just before serving.

Serves 4
No cooking
Use Mincer and Grating Attachments of Mixer or Grating Disc of Food Processor

450–550 g (1–1¼ lb) fillet steak
salt and pepper
4 eggs (yolks only used)
To garnish and flavour
large sprig parsley, 2 medium onions or 3
shallots, 2 tablespoons capers, 8–10
small gherkins

(MA) 1 Cut the meat into strips and mince, see page 49. Most people will prefer the meat if put through the fine plate, but this is a matter of personal taste.

(FP) Dice and chop the meat using the double-bladed cutting knife, see page 49.

2 Add salt and pepper when mincing or chopping the meat or when it is mixed at stage 8.
3 Form the meat into 4 flat cakes on a serving dish.
4 Crack the eggs and pour away the whites, these can be used in meringues, see page 89. Save half the egg shells.
5 Place each egg yolk in an egg shell half and place on the meat cakes.

(MA OR FP) 6 Chop the parsley in the mincer attachment or bowl of the food processor, using the double-bladed cutting knife. Transfer to a small bowl.

(MA OR FP) 7 Peel the onions and put through the grating (shredding) attachment of the mixer or grating disc of the food processor. You may prefer to dice the onions neatly by hand. Place in a bowl.

8 Place the capers and gherkins in bowls and arrange with the bowls of parsley and onion on the table with the meat. Each person takes their portion of meat, tips it into a bowl and adds as much or little of the garnish as desired. The meat is then mixed with an egg yolk, desired amount of garnish, salt and pepper.

9 Re-form into flat cakes and place on each serving plate. Serve with toast, bread and butter or crispbread and a salad.

To freeze
Do not freeze this dish. It is also better made with fresh, rather than frozen beef.

To vary
Add a little Worcestershire sauce to the meat mixture.

LIVER CUSTARD

Serves 3–4
Cooking time 1½ hours
Use Mincer Attachment of Mixer or Food Processor

4 chicken's liver
5 egg yolks or 3 eggs
450 ml (¾ pt) single cream
salt and pepper

(MA OR FP) 1 Mince or chop the livers very finely, see page 49.
2 Blend with the other ingredients.
3 Brush a 1-litre (1¾-pt) mould with a little oil and spoon in the mixture.
4 Stand the mould in a 'bain marie', (ovenproof container of cold water) and bake in the centre of a cool oven, 150°C, 300°F, Gas Mark 2, for about 1½ hours until firm. Turn out carefully and serve with hot toast and butter.

SAVOURY CUTLETS

Serves 4
Cooking time 12–15 minutes
Use Blender or Food Processor

8 lamb cutlets
salt and pepper
enough parsley to give 1 tablespoon
when chopped
1 small onion
50 g (2 oz) bread (weight without crusts)
1 tablespoon flour
1–2 eggs
little oil or fat

1 Trim the cutlets, removing any excess fat, and season with a little salt and pepper. Wash and dry the parsley on absorbent paper. Peel and quarter the onion.

55

B OR **FP**

2 Chop the bread, parsley and onion in the blender goblet or bowl of the food processor, using the double-bladed cutting knife; do not over-blend or over-process as the mixture will become too moist from the juice of the onion. See also Stuffings pages 76–78.

3 Tip the breadcrumb mixture on to a flat dish.

4 Mix the flour with a little salt and pepper, and coat the cutlets with this.

5 Beat the egg(s), brush over the cutlets, then roll the lamb in the breadcrumb mixture.

6 Heat enough oil or fat in a large frying pan to give a depth of 1 cm (½ in). Fry the coated cutlets for 6–7 minutes on each side. Drain on absorbent paper and garnish with cutlet frills. Serve with Apple Sauce or Barbecue Sauce and Vegetable Risotto, see pages 75, 52.

To freeze
Coat the cutlets, open freeze, then wrap. Cook from the frozen state.
   You can fry the cutlets, drain them, then open freeze and wrap. Use within 3 months.

To vary
Add a little mint instead of parsley to the bread.

1 Dice the meat. Squeeze out the lemon juice (you can use the juice extractor of the mixer or food processor). Peel and quarter the onions and apple.

MA OR **FP**

2 Fix the slicing attachment of the mixer or slicing disc of the food processor and press the onions and apple through with the pusher.

3 Heat the butter in a large saucepan, add the lamb, onions and apple and fry gently for about 5 minutes.

4 Add the curry powder, curry paste and chilli powder, if using this; fry gently for 2–3 minutes.

5 Stir in the flour, then the tomatoes, liquid from the can, stock, sultanas, chutney, lemon juice and salt and pepper.

6 Bring the mixture to the boil. Cover the pan, lower the heat and simmer gently for 1½ hours. Add a little extra stock during cooking if necessary, but this should be a fairly thick curry. If preferred, transfer to a preheated electric casserole. Cook on HIGH for 30 minutes, then on LOW for 6–8 hours.

7 Serve with boiled rice and bowls of sliced bananas, sliced tomatoes, raw onion rings and peanuts; use the slicing attachment of the mixer or slicing disc of the food processor to slice these accompaniments.

LAMB CURRY

(Illustrated on page 65)

Serves 4–6
Cooking time See method, stage 6
Use Slicing Attachment of Mixer *or* Slicing Disc of Food Processor

675 g (1½ lb) lamb (cut from the shoulder)
½ lemon
2 large onions
1 large cooking apple
50 g (2 oz) butter
1 tablespoon curry powder
2 teaspoons curry paste
1 teaspoon chilli powder (optional)
2 teaspoons flour
396 g (14 oz) can tomatoes
300 ml (½ pt) lamb or beef stock
50 g (2 oz) sultanas
2 tablespoons chutney
salt and pepper

Using cooked meats

One of the great benefits of owning a mincer attachment for an electric mixer or having a food processor is that you can use up cooked meats, poultry and game in interesting ways. A variety of recipes follows, with suggestions for varying the basic dish. You can, of course, make your own adaptations according to the foods you wish to use.

CURRIED CHICKEN MOUSSE

Serves 4–6 as a main course, 8 as an hors d'oeuvre
Cooking time about 5 mins
Use Mincer Attachment of Mixer and Mixer
or Food Processor and Mixer

350 g (12 oz) cooked chicken
15 g (½ oz) gelatine
2 tablespoons dry sherry or water
300 ml (½ pt) chicken stock or water and ½
   chicken stock cube
1 teaspoon curry paste or powder
few drops Tabasco sauce
1 teaspoon tomato purée
3 eggs
salt and pepper

To garnish
lettuce, tomatoes, cucumber

(MA) 1 Put the chicken through the fine or coarse plate of the mincer (depending upon personal taste).

(FP) Place the double-bladed cutting knife and bowl in position. Add the chicken, fix the lid and switch on for a few seconds.

2 Soften the gelatine in the cold sherry or water in a small bowl. Stand the bowl over a pan of hot water and leave until the gelatine has dissolved.

3 Heat the chicken stock or water and stock cube, add the dissolved gelatine, curry paste or powder, Tabasco sauce and tomato purée. Add the chopped chicken to the warm mixture. This gives a pleasantly moist texture to the poultry.

4 Separate the eggs, put the yolks into a fairly large bowl.

(M) 5 Use the whisk(s) and beat the egg yolks until thick and creamy. Gradually add the gelatine and chicken mixture, together with a little salt and pepper to taste.

(FP) It is not possible to whisk egg yolks until thick; this must be done by hand if a mixer is not available. Proceed as for mixer above.

6 Allow the mixture to stiffen very slightly.

(M) (OR) (FP) 7 Whisk the egg whites on high speed until stiff (some food processors can do this).

8 Gently fold the egg whites into the chicken mixture with a metal spoon.

9 Transfer to an oiled 1-litre (1¾-pt) mould and leave to set.

10 Turn out and garnish with the lettuce, thinly sliced tomatoes and cucumber slices.

(MA) (OR) (FP) The latter can be prepared with the slicing attachment of the mixer or slicing disc of the food processor.

11 Serve with mayonnaise, see recipe page 71.

To freeze
This mousse freezes well for up to 3 months.

To vary
CREAMY CHICKEN MOUSSE Use only a generous 150 ml (¼ pt) chicken stock or water and ¼ chicken stock cube. Continue to the end of stage 5. Add 3 tablespoons thick mayonnaise and allow the mixture to stiffen slightly. Whip 5 tablespoons double cream until it holds its shape, fold into the chicken mixture, then the egg whites.

HAM MOUSSE Use minced or chopped ham instead of chicken.

SALMON MOUSSE Use flaked cooked or canned salmon instead of chicken. Add a little lemon juice instead of all the water or sherry. Omit the curry flavouring.

LAMB SANDWICH FILLING

Fills 20–25 sandwiches
No cooking
Use Mincer and Grating Attachments of Mixer or Food Processor

225 g (8 oz) cooked lamb
100 g (4 oz) celery
100 g (4 oz) Cheddar cheese
100 g (4 oz) cucumber
2 tablespoons mayonnaise
½ teaspoon garlic salt
salt and pepper
chilli sauce to taste

(MA) 1 Cut the meat into strips and put through the fine or coarse plate (screen) of the mincer. Transfer to a bowl.

(FP) Dice the meat. Place the double-bladed cutting knife and bowl in position. Add the meat, fix the lid and switch on for a few seconds until the meat is chopped as finely as liked. Remove from the bowl, but replace the cutting knife unless you prefer to use the grating disc, see stage 3.

2 Dice the celery, cheese and cucumber.

(MA) 3 Replace the mincer with the grating attachment. Feed the celery, cheese and cucumber through in this order with the more moist ingredient added last. (If preferred mince all these ingredients together, after mincing the meat, it is less trouble but produces a softer mixture.)

(FP) Put the celery, cheese and cucumber into the bowl of the food processor, fix the lid and switch on for a few seconds; take care not to over-process. (If preferred you could use the grating disc and put the celery, then the cheese and finally the cucumber through this. It is more trouble, but gives a slightly better appearance to the ingredients.)

4 Mix all the ingredients together, add the hot chilli sauce gradually. Store in a covered container in the refrigerator until ready to use.

To freeze
This particular filling does not freeze well; refrigerate for ½–1 day only.

To vary
Chop or grate a little dessert apple with the other ingredients.

BEEF SANDWICH FILLING Use minced or chopped cooked beef instead of lamb, with only 1 tablespoon mayonnaise and 1 tablespoon horseradish cream.

CHICKEN SANDWICH FILLING Use minced or chopped cooked chicken instead of lamb, and omit the chilli sauce. Add a few drops of soy sauce. Turkey could be used.

DUCK SANDWICH FILLING Use minced or chopped cooked duck instead of lamb. Add a little chopped sage.

Potted foods

These smooth spreads can be served instead of pâté or as a sandwich filling or topping for hot toast.

After mincing, as stage 1, pound the ingredients together. A blender or food processor enables you to achieve the same result with very little effort.

POTTED MEAT

Select about 450 g (1 lb) lean cooked ham or equal quantities of veal and ham or very good quality beef, such as sirloin, rib or fillet. Melt 75 g (3 oz) butter; put 25 g (1 oz) on one side to cover the potted meat.

(MA) 1 Dice the meat and put through the fine plate (screen) of the mincer, then blend with 50 g (2 oz) butter, a little salt, pepper, pinch ground mace and 2 tablespoons sherry.

(B OR FP) 2 If using a blender or food processor, blend or process the diced meat with the 50 g (2 oz) butter and other ingredients given in stage 1.

3 Spoon into a container and top with the 25 g (1 oz) melted butter.

To freeze
Potted meat can be frozen for up to 1 month.

To vary
Use cooked game, poultry or fish instead of meat.

LAMB COTTAGE LOAF

Serves 4–6
Cooking time 40–50 mins
Use Mincer and Slicing Attachments of Mixer *or* Food Processor and Slicing Disc of Food Processor

225 g (8 oz) cooked lamb
1 medium onion
50 g (2 oz) mushrooms
1 small green pepper
396 g (14 oz) can tomatoes or 6 fresh tomatoes
25 g (1 oz) butter
salt and pepper
1 large round loaf or the base of a cottage loaf
225 g (8 oz) Bel Paese cheese

1 Dice the lamb. Peel and quarter the onion. Wipe the mushrooms. Remove the core and seeds from the pepper, dice the flesh. Chop the canned tomatoes or fresh tomatoes with a knife; do not use the liquid from the can.

2 Note the order of frying, stages 3 and 4, and keep the ingredients separated.

(MA) Put the meat, then the onion through the coarse plate (screen) of the mincer.

Mince the mushrooms and pepper, slice by hand or use the slicing attachment (also needed at stage 6).

FP Place the double-bladed cutting knife and bowl in position. Add the meat, fix the lid and switch on for a few seconds to chop the meat; remove from the bowl. Add and chop the onion then the pepper and mushrooms, or slice with the slicing disc.

3 Heat the butter in a frying pan, add the onion and green pepper and fry until soft.

4 Add the mushrooms, tomatoes, salt and pepper to taste.

5 Cut a slice from one end of the loaf and pull out the crumb part, leaving about 1 cm ($\frac{1}{2}$ in) bread all round the inside of the loaf. The unused bread can be used in various ways, i.e. soft or crisp breadcrumbs or in a pudding, see pages 28, 67.

MA OR FP 6 Put the cheese through the slicing attachment of the mixer or slicing disc of the food processor.

7 Place half the cheese and then half the lamb inside the loaf.

8 Cover the meat with half the tomato mixture; add the rest of the lamb and finally the remaining tomato mixture.

9 Cover the top of the outside of the loaf with the remaining sliced cheese.

10 Bake in the centre of a moderate oven, 180°C, 350°F, Gas Mark 4, for 30–40 minutes. Serve with salad.

To freeze
Prepare to the end of stage 10. Use within 1 month. Defrost before reheating.

To vary
Use other cooked meat in place of lamb.
Mince or chop 1 or 2 peeled cloves garlic and fry with the onions at stage 3.

SAMOSAS

(Illustrated on page 65)

Serves 4–6
Cooking time 18–20 mins
Use Mincer Attachment of Mixer *or* Food Processor

For the filling
225 g (8 oz) cooked lamb
1 medium onion
1 tablespoon oil
1–2 teaspoons curry powder
1 tablespoon chutney
salt and pepper

For the pastry
175 g (6 oz) self-raising flour or plain flour and 1½ teaspoons baking powder
pinch salt
85 g* (3 oz) shredded suet

For frying
deep oil or fat
*Use this metrication

MA 1 Cut the lamb into strips and put through the coarse plate (screen) of the mincer. Transfer to a bowl. Peel and quarter the onion, put through the mincer.

FP Dice the meat. Place the double-bladed cutting knife and bowl in position. Add the meat, fix the lid and switch on for 2–3 seconds until the meat is coarsely chopped; remove from the bowl. Peel and quarter the onion, chop fairly finely.

2 Heat the oil in a frying pan and fry the onion and curry powder for 5 minutes, stir during this period.

3 Add the minced lamb, cook gently for another 5 minutes, then add the chutney and a little salt and pepper.

4 Mix well and allow to cool completely.

5 Sift the flour, or flour and baking powder, and salt into a mixing bowl. Add the suet and blend together. Gradually add enough water to make a soft rolling consistency. This could be produced in the mixer or food processor. If you prefer to use butcher's suet, either put it through the mincer or chop and mix it with the flour in the food processor.

6 Roll out the pastry and cut into about twelve 10-cm (4-in) rounds.

7 Place a small amount of the meat mixture in the centre of each pastry round, damp the edges of the pastry and seal to form pasty shapes, as shown in the picture on page 65.

8 Heat the oil or fat to 170°C, 338°F, or until a cube of day-old bread turns golden within 1 minute.

9 Deep fry the pasties steadily for approximately 8 minutes or until firm and golden brown. Drain on absorbent paper and serve hot or cold.

To freeze
These are better eaten when freshly cooked.

To vary
Use other cooked meat, poultry or game for the filling.

Frying pastry

It makes a pleasant change to fry instead of bake a pastry case. It is very important though to make quite certain that the oil or fat is not too hot, otherwise the pastry becomes over-brown before it and the filling are adequately cooked. Do not shorten the recommended cooking time.

Quick ideas with cooked meats

These recipes and those on the previous page are ideal for quick snacks or light meals. The foods should be put through the mincer attachment of a mixer using the coarse plate, or chopped in the food processor, using the double-bladed cutting knife.

BEEF FRIED SANDWICHES Mince or chop 225 g (8 oz) cooked beef. Mix with a little chutney, made mustard and tomato ketchup. Cut 8–10 large slices of bread, spread with butter or margarine and make sandwiches with the beef. Cut each sandwich into 2 triangles. Beat 1 egg with 3 tablespoons milk, salt and pepper to taste. Dip each sandwich into the egg and milk rapidly so that the bread does not become over-soft. Heat 50–75 g (2–3 oz) fat or butter in a large frying pan. Fry the sandwiches for about 2 minutes or until crisp and golden on both sides. Serve at once. Makes 8–10 triangles.

Use the same filling in toasted sandwiches. Substitute other meats.

BEEF FRITTERS Make a thick batter by blending 100 g (4 oz) self-raising flour or plain flour with 1 teaspoon baking powder, pinch salt, cayenne or black pepper, mustard powder, 1 egg and 150 ml ($\frac{1}{4}$ pt)

milk. Mince or chop 175–225 g (6–8 oz) cooked beef, 1 peeled onion and a little parsley. Add to the batter and mix well. Heat 50–75 g (2–3 oz) fat in a frying pan. Fry spoonfuls of the mixture for 2 minutes or until golden on the under side. Turn and fry for the same time on the second side. Lower the heat and cook for a further 3–4 minutes until quite firm. Drain on absorbent paper. Serve hot or cold.
Makes about 12

STUFFED TOMATOES Mince or chop 175 g (6 oz) cooked meat, poultry or game and 1$\frac{1}{2}$ tablespoons mixed parsley, chives and tarragon. Cut a slice from 4 very large tomatoes. Scoop out and chop the tomato pulp, add the meat or poultry, herbs, 1 egg, salt and pepper. Spoon the mixture into the tomato cases and top with the tomato slices. Place in a buttered ovenproof dish and bake above the centre of a moderately hot oven, 190°C, 375°F, Gas Mark 5, for 15 minutes.
Serves 4

RISSOLES

This name is given to fried round cakes, made from cooked meat, poultry or game. Use the mincer or food processor or even the blender for small amounts. These serve 4.

1   Dice 350 g (12 oz) cooked meat, game or poultry and 50 g (2 oz) bread; you can use the crusts in this recipe.

(MA) 2   Put the meat through the coarse or fine plate (screen) of the mincer, then mince the bread.

FP   Place the double-bladed cutting knife and bowl in position. Add the meat and bread to the bowl, fix the lid and switch on for a few seconds until chopped as liked; leave in the bowl.

3   Make a thick White Sauce or Brown Sauce as pages 70 and 68; using 25 g (1 oz) butter or dripping, 25 g (1 oz) flour and 150 ml ($\frac{1}{4}$ pt) milk or stock.

M 4   Tip the minced meat and crumbs into the sauce, season to taste.

FP   Tip the sauce on to the meat, add salt and pepper to taste, fix the lid and switch on for 2–3 seconds.

5   Allow the mixture to cool and form into 8 round cakes. Coat in seasoned flour, then in beaten egg and crisp breadcrumbs.

6   Heat approximately 50 g (2 oz) fat in a frying pan and fry the rissoles until crisp and brown on each side. Drain on absorbent paper. Serve with Potato Chips, below.

To freeze
Open freeze, then wrap. Use within 3 months.

To vary
CURRIED CUTLETS Peel and mince or chop 2 onions and 2 cloves garlic. Increase the fat at stage 3 to 50 g (2 oz), fry the onions and garlic until tender and add 1–2 tablespoons curry powder. Continue as stages 3 and 4 but add 1 tablespoon chutney and 1 tablespoon desiccated coconut to the ingredients. Form into cutlet shapes, coat and fry.

CROQUETTES Prepare the basic mixture or one made from these variations into finger shapes and deep fry.
Peel and chop 1–2 onions and 2 tomatoes; fry in extra fat at stage 3 before making the sauce. Add chopped fresh herbs to taste.

POTATO CHIPS

Serves 4
Cooking time 8–12 mins
Use Potato Chip Disc of Food Processor

0.75 kg (1½ lb) potatoes
oil or fat for frying

1   Peel the potatoes, cut into convenient shapes to fit the feed-tube of the food processor. Keep in cold water until ready to cut into chip shapes.
2   Place the potato chip disc in position. Dry the potatoes on absorbent paper.
FP 3   Push the potatoes through the feed-tube, the harder you press the potatoes with the pusher the thicker the chips will be. Dry the chips again before frying.
4   Put enough oil or fat into a deep saucepan to come half way up the sides. Never exceed this amount because when the potatoes are put into the pan they cause the oil or fat to over flow. If using one of the new electric fryers, fill with oil to the level marked by the

manufacturer. Heat the oil or fat to 150–160°C, 300–320°F, or if the chips are thin, produced by most food processor discs, the temperature can be raised to 170°C, 338–340°F. To test without a thermometer, put in a cube of day-old bread or a single chip. The bread should turn golden within ½ minute; the chip should rise to the top of the oil or fat. Heat the basket in the oil or fat; this prevents food sticking to the mesh.
5   Half fill the basket with the chips; fry for 5–10 minutes, or until tender.
6   Remove the potatoes from the pan. Reheat the oil or fat to 190°C, 375°F, if testing with a cube of bread or a chip it should start to cook immediately. Replace the chips, fry for 2 minutes or until crisp and brown. Drain on absorbent paper.

To vary
SLICED POTATOES Use the slicing attachment of the mixer or slicing disc of the food processor. Fry as Potato Chips above.

Classic minced meat dishes

The following three recipes each serve 4 people and can be prepared in large amounts, for the cooked dish freezes well for up to 3 months. Advice for mincing or processing meat is given on page 49 and details of preparing vegetables on page 79. The traditional choice of meat is given in each recipe, but other meats could be used instead.
I have also given a recipe for a Chicken Terrine, this is an appetizing blend of sliced and minced poultry.

BOLOGNESE SAUCE

1   Peel 1 large onion, 1 clove garlic and 2 medium carrots. Wipe but do not peel 50 g (2 oz) mushrooms.

(MA) 2   Put 450 g (1 lb) good quality stewing steak through the coarse plate (screen) of the mincer, then mince the prepared vegetables.

(FP)   Cut the vegetables into pieces. Place the double-bladed cutting knife and bowl in position. Add the vegetables, fix the lid and switch on for a few seconds to chop. Remove, add 450 g (1 lb) good quality stewing steak and chop.

3   Heat 1 tablespoon oil and 25 g (1 oz) butter in a strong saucepan, add all the vegetables and the meat and cook gently until they are lightly coloured, stirring well.

4   Skin and chop 2 tomatoes, add to the mixture with 450 ml (¾ pt) beef stock or use a mixture of red wine and stock. Add salt and pepper to taste.

5   Stir briskly to break up any lumps of meat, then allow the sauce to simmer gently for about 45 minutes, until the surplus liquid has evaporated and the meat and vegetables are tender.

6   Stir frequently, especially towards the end of the cooking time. Serve with cooked spaghetti or other pasta or rice.

CHILLI CON CARNE

(Illustrated on page 65)

1   Peel and quarter 2 medium onions. Slice 225 g (8 oz) tomatoes with a knife.

(MA) 2   Put 450 g (1 lb) stewing steak through the coarse plate (screen) of the mincer, then mince the onions.

(FP)   Place the double-bladed cutting knife and bowl in position. Add the onions, fix the lid and switch on for a few seconds to chop; remove from the bowl. Add 450 g (1 lb) stewing steak and chop.

3   Heat 50 g (2 oz) fat or dripping in a saucepan, add the beef and onions and stir over a low heat for 5 minutes.

4   Gradually stir in 1 tablespoon chilli powder (add this very slowly, as it is very hot); add the tomatoes and cook for a further 5 minutes.

5   Pour in 300 ml (½ pt) beef stock, add a little salt and pepper, stir well and cover the pan. Simmer for 40 minutes, stirring several times to prevent the

thick stew from burning; if necessary add a little extra stock.

6   Tip in a 396 g (14 oz) can red kidney beans, blend well with the meat and cook for a further 10 minutes.

MOUSSAKA

1   Wipe 2 medium aubergines. Peel 4 medium potatoes and 2 medium onions.

(MA OR FP) 2   Put the vegetables through the slicing attachment of the mixer or slicing disc of a food processor; keep the onions separate. Slice 4 medium tomatoes with a knife.

3   Heat 1 tablespoon oil and 25 g (1 oz) butter in a pan, add the aubergines and potatoes and fry for 10 minutes; remove from the pan. Heat another 1 tablespoon oil and 25 g (1 oz) butter in the pan; add the onions and tomatoes and fry for 10 minutes until the onions are soft.

(MA OR FP) 4   Fix the mincer attachment of the mixer and put 450 g (1 lb) lean lamb through the coarse plate (screen) or chop in the food processor, using the double-bladed cutting knife; mix with the onions and tomatoes.

5   Make 300 ml (½ pt) Cheese Sauce, see page 70, add 1 beaten egg and a little grated nutmeg.

6   Put a third of the aubergines and potatoes into a 1.8-litre (3-pt) casserole. Adding a little salt and pepper and sauce to each layer, cover with half the meat mixture, a further layer of aubergines and potatoes, the last of the meat mixture and a final topping of aubergines.

7   Cover the casserole and bake in the centre of a moderate oven, 160°C, 325°F, Gas Mark 3, for 1½ hours.

CHICKEN TERRINE

Serves 6
Cooking time 2½ hours
Use Mincer Attachment of Mixer *or* Food
Processor

**1 large roasting chicken about 2.25 kg (5
  lb)**
50 g (2 oz) bread
**enough fresh parsley to give 1
  tablespoon when chopped**
1 onion
1 bay leaf
1 sprig of thyme
salt and pepper
4 tablespoons chicken stock (see method)
4 tablespoons double cream
2 egg yolks
To coat
1 packet of aspic jelly to set 600 ml (1 pt)

1   Cut all the breast meat from the chicken
    in thick pieces; cover to prevent drying
    while preparing the rest of the mixture.
2   Cut away all the rest of the chicken
    flesh from the body and legs.
3   Put the dark flesh through the fine plate
    (screen) of the mincer, then mince the
    bread and parsley.
    Place the double-bladed cutting knife
    and bowl in position. Add the dark
    flesh, bread and parsley, fix the lid and
    switch on for a few seconds until finely
    chopped.
4   Put the chicken bones with the whole
    peeled onion, bay leaf, thyme and a
    very little salt and pepper (do not over-
    season as the stock will be used with a
    highly seasoned aspic jelly) into a
    saucepan. Add water to cover and
    simmer for at least 1 hour, then strain
    the liquid; use at stages 6 and 9.
5   Slice the breast meat.
6   Mix the minced meat and breadcrumb
    mixture with the 4 tablespoons of stock,
    cream and egg yolks.
7   Put layers of minced and sliced chicken
    into a buttered round casserole or
    terrine mould, beginning and ending
    with a minced layer.
8   Stand in a roasting tin or similar
    container of cold water and bake in the
    centre of a moderate oven, 160°C, 325°F
    Gas Mark 3, for 1½ hours. Turn out and
    allow to cool.
9   Dissolve the aspic jelly in the strained
    chicken stock. Allow to cool and
    become slightly thickened. Use about
    half to coat the terrine, leave to become

firm. Let the rest of the jelly set. Place
the terrine on a bed of mixed salad.
Whisk or chop the remaining jelly and
spoon round the edge of the dish.

To freeze
Freeze the terrine without the aspic
coating. Use within 3 months. Defrost and
complete stage 9.

To vary
CHICKEN AND HAM TERRINE Mince or
chop 50–100 g (2–4 oz) blanched almonds
with the chicken. Mince or chop 225 g
(8 oz) lean ham with the chicken.

GAME TERRINE Use 2 young pheasants or
grouse instead of chicken.

HAM AND TONGUE PÂTÉ

This can be served as a main dish. It
combines minced and diced meats. **In this,
as all recipes using the food processor,
never chop more than the recommended
amount at one time – do it in batches.**

1   Coarsely dice 450 g (1 lb) cooked ham
    or boiled bacon and 225 g (8 oz) cooked
    tongue. Sprig enough parsley to give 2
    tablespoons when chopped. Wash 4
    spring onions.
2   Finely chop the ham, parsley and
    onions in the blender goblet or bowl of
    the food processor, using the double-
    bladed cutting knife.
3   Drop some of the tongue through the
    'hole' in the blender lid or feed-tube
    when each batch of ham etc. is nearly
    ready; chop for 1–2 seconds only so the
    tongue remains in pieces.
4   Make a purée of 175 g (6 oz) tomatoes in
    the blender goblet or bowl of the food
    processor, using the double-bladed
    cutting knife. Bind the meat mixture
    with this and season to taste. Press into
    a basin and leave for 1 hour to form a
    shape.

Serves 4–6

To freeze
This pâté freezes for up to 6 weeks.

To vary
Add 25 g (1 oz) melted butter and 1
tablespoon cream for a moister mixture.

63

CHAPTER 7
CHEESE DISHES

There are many recipes in which cheese is an important ingredient. There are many ways of preparing cheese for various dishes.

To chop cheese
Use either the blender or food processor, using the double-bladed cutting knife. Dice the cheese, put into the blender goblet or bowl of the food processor. Fix the lid and switch on until the cheese is chopped; do not over-blend or over-process, otherwise the cheese becomes sticky.

To grate cheese
Use the grating attachment of the mixer or grating disc of a food processor (these are often referred to as a shredding or chopping attachment or disc). Feed the cheese through with the pusher. The grated cheese looks good on salads.

To slice cheese
Use the slicing attachment of a mixer or slicing disc of a food processor. Feed the cheese through with the pusher. The cheese is neatly sliced for salads, sandwich fillings, toasted cheese, etc.

To blend cheese that is unsuitable for grating is shown in the Party Dips on this page.

Ways to use grated cheese

SPEEDY RAREBIT Grate 225 g (8 oz) Cheddar cheese. Blend with 25 g (1 oz) butter, 1 teaspoon made mustard, 1 teaspoon Worcestershire sauce, 1 egg, salt and pepper. Spread on 4 slices of buttered toast. Heat and lightly brown under the grill. Serves 4

Party dips

A good dip should have the consistency of whipped cream. Serve it in a bowl with salad ingredients, cooked sausages, biscuits and crisps around the bowl.

You can prepare a smooth mixture in seconds with the aid of the blender or food processor, using the double-bladed cutting knife.

Each recipe given below serves 4–6 if you are serving just one mixture but obviously there will be sufficient for many more people if you are making a selection of dips. More recipes are on page 21.

BLUE CHEESE AND NUT DIP Blue cheese is inclined to cling to the blades of a blender or food processor, so just chop 100 g (4 oz) nuts in the blender goblet or bowl of the food processor. Blend with 225 g (8 oz) blue cheese and 2–3 tablespoons cream.

PINEAPPLE AND CHEESE DIP Dice 225 g (8 oz) Cheddar, Edam or Gouda cheese. Place in the blender goblet or bowl of the food processor. Switch on until finely chopped. Add 6 tablespoons single cream and switch on for a few seconds more. Open a small can pineapple rings, drain and quarter these; add through the hole in the lid of the blender, see page 11, or feed-tube of the food processor, with the machine in operation. Leave for a few seconds until finely chopped.

Transform an ordinary dish into an exotic one with the addition of spices to your cooking
Chilli Con Carne (page 62), Samosas (page 59), Lamb Curry (page 56)

CHEESE AND HADDOCK SOUFFLÉ

Serves 4
Cooking time 45–50 mins
Use Grating Attachment of Mixer and
Mixer *or* Blender *or* Food Processor

**175 g (6 oz) smoked haddock (weight
  without bones)**
75 g (3 oz) Cheddar cheese
25 g (1 oz) butter
25 g (1 oz) flour
¾ teaspoon mustard powder
**¾ teaspoon chopped fresh or pinch dried
  marjoram**
200 ml (7 fl oz) milk
3 eggs
salt and pepper

1 Grease a 15–18-cm (6–7-in) soufflé dish.
2 Put about 300 ml (½ pt) water into a
   saucepan, add the haddock and poach
   for about 6–7 minutes until just tender,
   do not over-cook. If using frozen
   haddock in a 'boil in the bag' container
   follow the packet instructions. Drain and
   flake the fish.
3 Grate the cheese as the instructions on
   page 64.
4 Heat the butter in a large saucepan, stir
   in the flour, mustard and marjoram and
   cook over a low heat for 1 minute.
5 Remove the pan from the heat and
   gradually add the milk. Bring to the boil
   and cook until a thick sauce, stirring all
   the time.
6 Separate the eggs.

M   Put the whites into the mixer bowl
   and whisk until just stiff, using a high
   speed.

FP   Some processors have a double-
   bladed chopping knife that will whisk
   egg whites; if this is possible put the
   whites into the bowl with the double-
   bladed knife. Fix the lid and switch on
   until just stiff.
      Alternatively whisk in a mixer or use
   a hand whisk.
7 Blend the egg yolks, haddock, cheese,
   a little salt and pepper with the sauce,
   then fold in the egg whites.
8 Spoon the mixture into the soufflé dish
   and bake in the centre of a moderately
   hot oven, 190°C, 375°F, Gas Mark 5, for
   about 35 minutes or until well risen and
   firm. Serve at once.

To freeze
Do not freeze.

CRUMB QUICHE

Serves 4–6
Cooking time 50–55 mins
Use Mixer and Blender *or* Food Processor

**pastry made with 175 g (6 oz) flour etc.
  (see page 84)**
For the filling
50 g (2 oz) bread (weight without crusts)
300 ml (½ pt) milk or single cream
75 g (3 oz) Cheddar cheese
1 small sprig parsley
3 eggs or 4 egg yolks
1 teaspoon Worcestershire sauce
salt and pepper

M
or
FP 1 Make the pastry in the mixer or food
   processor as page 84. Roll out and use
   to line a 20-cm (8-in) flan dish. Bake
   'blind' in a moderately hot oven, 200°C,
   400°F, Gas Mark 6, for 15 minutes.

B
or
FP 2 Make the bread into crumbs,
   see page 28, in the blender or food
   processor.
3 Heat the milk or cream, add the crumbs
   and allow to stand for a few minutes.

B
or
FP 4 Dice the cheese and grate in the
   blender or food processor with the
   parsley, see page 64.
5 Add the cheese, parsley, well beaten
   eggs or egg yolks, Worcestershire
   sauce, salt and pepper to the milk or
   cream and crumbs.
6 Spoon into the part baked pastry case.
   Lower the oven temperature to
   moderate, 160°C, 325°F, Gas Mark 3,
   and bake for 35–40 minutes or until set.
7 Serve hot or cold with salad.

To freeze
Freezes for 3 months, particularly when
cream is used. Open freeze, then wrap.

To vary
CRUMB QUICHE LORRAINE Chop 75 g
(3 oz) streaky or back bacon – this can be
done in a food processor or coarse mincer.
Fry for a few minutes until crisp, drain and
add to the other ingredients.

CLASSIC QUICHE Omit the breadcrumbs
and add chopped bacon.

STUFFED MUSHROOMS Wipe 6 large
mushrooms, remove the stalks; chop and
mix with 25 g (1 oz) fine breadcrumbs, 75 g
(3 oz) grated cheese, a little chopped
parsley, salt, pepper and 1 egg. Spoon on
to the underside of the mushrooms and
place in an ovenproof dish with 150 ml
(¼ pt) single cream. Cover and bake in the
centre of a moderate oven, 180°C, 350°F,
Gas Mark 4, for 35 minutes.

Using left-over foods

The term 'left-overs' usually sounds rather dreary. I regard the sight of stale bread, a portion of meat or fish too small to make a complete meal by itself, or an assortment of cooked vegetables, as an interesting challenge. Here are some ideas for using up these foods.

BREAD is expensive and no one likes to waste it. Left-over bread can be made into breadcrumbs and stuffings as pages 28, 76–78 . Breadcrumbs can be frozen for about 6 weeks.

It is easy to crisp breadcrumbs for coating foods. Spread the crumbs on flat baking trays and dry out in a cool oven, 140°C, 275°F, Gas Mark 1, for about 1–1½ hours. Put into the blender goblet or bowl of the food processor, using the double-bladed cutting knife, to produce very fine crumbs (check the manufacturer's instructions). Store in airtight jars or tins.

Add soft breadcrumbs to a steamed pudding mixture for a lighter result e.g. where a recipe states 175 g (6 oz) flour, use 150 g (5 oz) flour and 25 g (1 oz) soft breadcrumbs.

An old fashioned but very delicious pudding is based on breadcrumbs.

QUEEN OF PUDDINGS Make 50 g (2 oz) breadcrumbs as page 28 and put into a bowl. Heat 300 ml (½ pt) milk in a pan, separate 2 eggs, whisk the yolks into the milk and add 25 g (1 oz) sugar. Strain over the crumbs, add 1 teaspoon finely grated lemon rind and leave to stand. Spread 2 tablespoons jam or lemon curd in the base of a buttered 900-ml (1½-pt) pie dish, add the crumb mixture. Bake in the centre of a moderate oven, 160°C, 325°F, Gas Mark 3, for 40 minutes, or until firm. Spread with a little more jam or curd. Whisk the 2 egg whites until stiff and fold in 50 g (2 oz) caster sugar. Spoon the meringue over the pudding. Return to the oven for 20 minutes. Serve hot.
Serves 4

FISH can be made into fish cakes. Never keep cooked or canned fish for any length of time – even in a refrigerator.

FISH CAKES Flake cooked white fish or oily fish, such as mackerel or canned tuna or salmon. Cook and mash 225 g (8 oz) potatoes as page 81. Add approximately the same amount of fish plus 1 egg, a little salt, pepper and chopped parsley. The mixture can be blended for 1–2 seconds in a food processor but do *not* over-process as the mixture will become sticky. Form into 8 cakes, coat in seasoned flour, 1 beaten egg and 50 g (2 oz) crisp breadcrumbs.

Heat 50 g (2 oz) fat in a frying pan; fry the cakes on each side until crisp, brown and very hot. Drain on absorbent paper. Serve hot.
Serves 4

FRUIT can be made into a purée for desserts, see page 82, or Fresh Fruit Milk Shakes see page 18. Fruit purées can be frozen.

MEAT can be used in many ways, see pages 49 to 63.

VEGETABLES, like fruit, can be made into a purée and frozen. This is useful with a glut of tomatoes. Use the sieve and colander attachment of a mixer for a seedless purée, or use a blender or food processor. Pack the purée into containers and freeze for up to 6–8 months. Combine small amounts of left-over raw vegetables with cheese or cooked meat (especially ham) to make pasties.

SAVOURY PASTIES Make shortcrust pastry as page 84 using 350 g (12 oz) flour, pinch salt, 150–175 g (5–6 oz) fat, water to bind, in the mixer or food processor. Roll out to about 0.5 cm (¼ in) in thickness. Cut into 4–6 large rounds. Peel 2 large potatoes, 2 carrots, 2 medium onions, put through the slicing attachment of a mixer or slicing disc of a food processor. Blend with 2 skinned and chopped tomatoes, 100–175 g (4–6 oz) grated cheese or minced or chopped cooked meat. Add salt and pepper to taste. Spoon into the centre of the pastry rounds. Moisten the edges, seal and flute to form pasty shapes. Brush with beaten egg or milk to glaze and put on a baking tray. Bake in the centre of a moderately hot oven, 200°C, 400°F, Gas Mark 6, for 20 minutes, then reduce the heat to moderate 180°C, 350°F, Gas Mark 4, for a further 20–25 minutes.
Serves 4–6

CHAPTER 8

SAUCES AND STUFFINGS

Sauces and stuffings become so much easier and quicker to prepare with a blender, food processor or attachment of a mixer.

BROWN SAUCE

Serves 2–4 depending on the dish
Cooking time 20 mins
Use Slicing Attachment of Mixer and Blender *or* Slicing Disc of Food Processor and Food Processor

1 small onion
1 small carrot
50 g (2 oz) butter or dripping
25 g (1 oz) flour
450 ml (¾ pt) stock
salt and pepper

1 Peel the onion and carrot. Put through the slicing attachment of the mixer or slicing disc of the food processor.
2 Heat the butter or dripping in a pan, add the vegetables and cook gently for several minutes.
3 Stir the flour into the vegetable mixture. Heat gently until the flour turns golden brown; if too dark the sauce will taste bitter.
4 Gradually add the stock and bring to the boil, stirring until thickened. Add salt and pepper to taste. Cover the pan and simmer for 10 minutes.
5 Pour the sauce and vegetables into the warmed blender goblet or bowl of the food processor, using the double-bladed cutting knife. Fix the lid and switch on until smooth. Reheat if necessary.
   Serve with meat, poultry or game.

To freeze
Better served fresh but can be frozen for up to 3 months.

To vary
SIMPLE BROWN SAUCE Make as White Sauce page 70. Use brown stock instead of milk.

ESPAGNOLE SAUCE Chop and add 2 mushrooms, 2 tomatoes and 1 bacon rasher at stage 2. Add 2 tablespoons sherry, at stage 5, omitting 2 tablespoons of the stock.
   Use a little port, Madeira wine or tomato juice in place of some of the stock.

Smooth sauces

You will find a blender or food processor is excellent in producing a velvet-like smoothness to sauces.

Place the double-bladed cutting knife or the plastic knife and bowl in position. Pour the thickened sauce into the blender goblet or bowl of the food processor. Fix the blender or food processor lid and switch on. Use a low speed at the beginning when using the blender so that the mixture does not rise too rapidly, and then gradually increase the speed. Blend or process for a few seconds or until the mixture is absolutely smooth.

This method is the perfect answer for getting rid of a skin that may have formed on the sauce, or for making a slightly lumpy sauce into a perfectly smooth one. You will find the consistency a little thinner after

Serve a complimentary sauce with the main dish and make the meal complete
Roast Duck with Piquant Orange Sauce (page 74)

blending or processing. If the sauce is too thin for your requirements, pour the sauce back into the pan and allow it to cook a little longer. This makes the excess moisture evaporate and produces the original consistency; longer cooking often improves the flavour of a sauce.

WHITE SAUCE

White Sauce blends with savoury dishes.

Serves 2–4 depending on the recipe
Cooking time 10–12 mins
Use Blender *or* Food Processor

For a coating consistency
25 g (1 oz) butter or margarine
25 g (1 oz) flour
300 ml (½ pt) milk
salt and pepper

1 Heat the butter or margarine in a saucepan, remove from the heat. Add the flour and return to a low heat, stirring gently as the 'roux' (the fat and flour) forms a ball.
2 Stir in the milk and a little salt and pepper, bring to the boil.
3 Continue stirring and cooking until the sauce coats the back of the wooden spoon.
B **OR** **FP** 4 For an extra smooth sauce, see Smooth Sauces page 68.

To freeze
This sauce can be frozen for up to 3 months but is better freshly served.

To vary
THIN WHITE SAUCE Follow the method above but use 450–600 ml (¾–1 pt) milk.

THICK WHITE SAUCE (PANADA) Follow the method above but use 150 ml (¼ pt) milk.

QUICK WHITE SAUCE Put the fat, flour and milk into a saucepan, whisk vigorously (use a hand whisk or small portable whisk) as the mixture heats and thickens. Or mix all the ingredients in the blender or food processor, tip into a pan and cook as above.

SWEET WHITE SAUCE Use 15 g (½ oz) cornflour, no seasoning but 25–50 g (1–2 oz) sugar and any flavourings, i.e. vanilla, chocolate, etc.

BÉCHAMEL SAUCE Chop or slice a little onion, celery and carrot. Heat the milk and vegetables, cover the pan and allow to stand for 1 hour. Strain, discard the vegetables and make the sauce with the flavoured milk. You may need a little extra milk. Serve with most savoury dishes.

CREAMY VEGETABLE SAUCE Infuse the milk and vegetables as in Béchamel Sauce above, but blend or process the vegetables and milk. Make the sauce in the usual way. The vegetables will have added some thickening so either reduce the flour to 15 g (½ oz) or increase the liquid to 450 ml (¾ pt). Excellent with vegetables.

Based on White Sauce
There are many variations of the White or Béchamel Sauce. Make the sauce as the basic recipe, pour into the blender goblet or bowl of the food processor, using the double-bladed cutting knife, and proceed as the specific recipe.

When making the sauce to serve with vegetables use part milk and part vegetable stock, to serve with fish or chicken use half milk or single cream and half fish or chicken stock.

CHEESE SAUCE Select a good cooking cheese, i.e. Cheddar, Gruyère, Parmesan, etc. Use 50–100 g (2–4 oz) cheese and add a little mustard to the sauce. There are two ways of incorporating the cheese:
a) Dice the cheese. Pour the very hot sauce into the warmed blender goblet or bowl of the food processor, add the cheese, switch on until the cheese is incorporated into the sauce.
b) Grate the cheese as page 64. Add to the hot sauce in the saucepan and heat gently until the cheese has melted.
Serve with vegetables or savoury dishes.

MUSHROOM SAUCE Fry approximately 50 g (2 oz) mushrooms in 25 g (1 oz) butter. Add to the sauce, then blend or process.

PARSLEY SAUCE Flavour is lost if the parsley is chopped on a board. Chop and add it to the sauce in one of the following ways:
a) Add sprigs of parsley to the hot sauce in the blender goblet or bowl of the food processor. Blend or process until the parsley is chopped in the sauce.
b) Chop the parsley in the blender goblet

or bowl of the food processor, add to the sauce and mix.

Serve at once or return to the heat and cook for 2–3 minutes. By cooking the parsley, the flavour will be more mellow.

PRAWN SAUCE Add 50–100 g (2–4 oz) shelled prawns. If the prawns are large, blend or process with the sauce to give smaller pieces. Serve with fish.

VELOUTÉ SAUCE Whisk in 1 egg yolk and 2 tablespoons cream after stage 4; simmer for 2–3 minutes.

HOLLANDAISE SAUCE

The method of making this sauce varies according to the equipment used. The first way, using a small electric whisk, is the classic method. Obviously less effort is involved when using an electrical appliance, making the preparation of Hollandaise Sauce very much easier.

Make quite certain the egg mixture really has thickened before incorporating the butter. If it is just fluffy it will become thin again as it stands or cools.

Serves 4
Cooking time 10–15 minutes
Use Mixer

2 egg yolks
pinch cayenne pepper (optional)
salt and pepper
1–2 tablespoons lemon juice or white wine vinegar
50–100 g (2–4 oz) butter

1   Put the egg yolks, seasonings, half the lemon juice or vinegar into a bowl. Cut the butter into small pieces, leave in a warm place, but do not melt.

M 2   Balance the bowl over a saucepan of hot, but *not boiling*, water. Switch to the lowest speed and whisk the egg yolk mixture continuously until it begins to thicken.

M 3   When the mixture is really thick, gradually whisk in the butter, piece by piece; do not add too rapidly, otherwise the mixture will curdle. Gradually whisk in the rest of the lemon juice or vinegar if liked.
Serve hot over vegetables, hot or cold with fish.

The method of mixing is similar for a blender or food processor, using the same ingredients as above. You need to loosen the cap in the centre of the lid of a blender or make a foil lid if necessary, see page 11. Use the double-bladed cutting knife in the food processor.

1   Melt the butter; it must be at boiling point, but not allowed to darken.

B OR **FP** 2   Put the egg yolks, seasoning and most of the lemon juice or vinegar into the blender goblet or bowl of the food processor, using the double-bladed cutting knife.

B OR **FP** 3   Fix the lid and switch on for a few seconds until the ingredients are blended. Remove the cap or fix the funnel for the blender if necessary.

B OR **FP** 4   Make sure the blender is running at medium speed or the food processor is switched on; check that the butter is very hot.

B OR **FP** 5   Pour the butter in a slow steady stream through the hole in the blender lid or feed-tube of the food processor; the sauce will automatically thicken. Add the extra lemon juice or vinegar if liked.

To freeze
This freezes well for up to 1 month. Rewhisk when defrosted.

MAYONNAISE

Making mayonnaise is very similar to the process given for Hollandaise Sauce. You can use an electric whisk, but it is much easier if you use a blender or food processor. If you use a whisk only the egg yolks can be used; whereas in a blender or food processor you can use the whole eggs for a lighter dressing. Make sure the eggs and oil are both at room temperature before making the dressing.

Serves 4
No cooking
Use Mixer

2 egg yolks or 2 eggs (see above)
½ teaspoon mustard powder or 1 teaspoon French mustard
salt and pepper
up to 300 ml (½ pt) olive oil
1–2 tablespoons white wine vinegar or lemon juice

M 1   Put the egg yolks into a dry basin and

add the seasonings. Switch to the lowest speed, then gradually whisk in the oil, *drop by drop*, until the mayonnaise reaches the desired consistency and enough oil is added for your personal taste.

M 2 Whisk in the vinegar or lemon juice. About ½–1 tablespoon boiling water can then be whisked into the dressing for a lighter result.

When using the blender loosen the cap or make a foil lid, see page 11; use the double-bladed cutting knife in the food processor.

B or **FP** 1 Put the egg yolks or whole eggs into the blender goblet or bowl of the food processor, using the double-bladed cutting knife.

B or **FP** 2 Fix the lid and switch on for a few seconds. Remove the cap or fix the foil funnel for the blender if necessary.

B or **FP** 3 Make sure the blender is running at medium speed or the food processor is switched on; then start to add the oil. Pour in just a few drops to begin with, then pour the oil in a slow steady stream through the hole, in the blender lid or feed-tube of the food processor. Add the seasonings at this stage.

B or **FP** 4 When the sauce has thickened or you have added enough oil for your personal taste, add the vinegar or lemon juice. Boiling water can also be added as described in stage 2 of making mayonnaise with a mixer.

To freeze
Do not freeze.

To vary
ANCHOVY MAYONNAISE Add a few drops anchovy essence or several anchovy fillets if using the blender or food processor at stage 4. Omit the salt.

CHEESE MAYONNAISE Add a little blue cheese at stage 4, blend well.

CURRY MAYONNAISE Add 1 teaspoon curry paste at stage 4.

LEMON MAYONNAISE Use the maximum amount of lemon juice in the dressing and add 1 teaspoon grated lemon 'zest'.

MARY ROSE DRESSING Blend 1 tablespoon fresh or concentrated tomato purée and a few drops of Worcestershire

sauce at stage 4. A little whipped cream can also be added to the completed mayonnaise.

TARTARE SAUCE If using a whisk, chop enough gherkins to give ½–1 tablespoon, parsley to give ½–1 tablespoon and capers to give 2 teaspoons. Add to the mayonnaise when thickened. If using a blender or food processor, drop the ingredients into the machine while in operation at the end of stage 4. Blend or process for a very brief time until chopped.

Fruit and vegetable sauces

A fruit sauce can be served with meat, poultry or sweet puddings. Do not use too much liquid in cooking the fruit or vegetables if the mixture is to be puréed in a blender or food processor. These produce a more liquid mixture than when sieving. For cooked sauces, see pages 68 to 71.

UNCOOKED CRANBERRY SAUCE

Serves 6
No cooking
Use Blender *or* Food Processor

1 large orange
225 g (8 oz) cranberries
175 g (6 oz) caster sugar

1 Cut the unpeeled orange into thick slices and remove all the pips. Wash and dry the cranberries.

B 2 Put some of the cranberries and sugar into the blender goblet. Put on the lid and switch to medium, then high speed until a little juice runs from the fruit. Remove the centre cap from the lid, or replace the lid with a foil cover with a centre hole, or with a foil funnel, see page 11. Switch on to medium speed and drop a few orange slices into the goblet through the hole or funnel; leave until the orange is finely chopped. Tip

Home-made ice cream is an ideal dessert for convenience as it can be made in advance and served anytime
Coffee and Ginger Ice Cream (page 84)

the prepared sauce out of the goblet and continue blending the rest of the fruit and sugar.

FP Place the double-bladed cutting knife and bowl in position. Add all the cranberries and all the sugar, fix the lid and switch on for a few seconds until the juice begins to flow. Push the orange slices through the feed-tube with the pusher while the machine is in operation, leave for about 15 seconds or until the orange is finely chopped. Serve without cooking.

To freeze
This freezes well and can be kept for up to 1 year.

ORANGE SAUCE

Serves 4–6
Cooking time 25 mins
Use Bean and Citrus Peel Slicer and Juice Extractor Attachments of Mixer *or* Slicing Disc and Juice Extractor of Food Processor

2 large oranges
150 ml (¼ pt) water
300 ml (½ pt) stock*
2 teaspoons arrowroot
1 teaspoon lemon juice
1–2 teaspoons sugar
salt and pepper

*Made from simmering duck or goose giblets in water.

1 Cut away the 'zest' (orange part of the peel) from the oranges; discard the white pith, which would make the sauce over-bitter.
MA OR FP 2 Put the peel through the bean and citrus peel slicer of the mixer or the slicing disc of the food processor.
3 Pour the water into a saucepan and add the shredded orange peel. Cover the pan and simmer for about 15 minutes or until the peel is tender. You can shorten the cooking time slightly if the peel is allowed to soak for 1–2 hours in the water.
MA OR FP 4 Fix the juice extractor, halve the oranges and extract the juice; or use a hand lemon squeezer.
5 Blend the stock with the arrowroot and add to the orange peel with the orange and lemon juices, sugar, salt and

pepper. Stir over the heat until the sauce thickens.
    Serve with duck or goose.

To freeze
This sauce freezes well. Use within 6 months.

To vary
Add 2 tablespoons redcurrant jelly.

PIQUANT ORANGE SAUCE
(*Illustrated on page 69*)
Make a gravy or Brown Sauce as page 68 but use slightly less duck giblet stock. Add 2 tablespoons orange juice, 2 tablespoons port wine and 2 tablespoons redcurrant jelly. Stir until smooth and thickened.

Sauces for slimmers

Spiced Tomato Sauce is a good example of a low calorie sauce as it contains no thickening ingredient. Adapt this idea and make a purée of cooked or raw vegetables in the blender or food processor, e.g. carrots and/or red and green pepper with tomatoes. Make fruit sauces and sweeten with sugar substitute.

SPICED TOMATO SAUCE

Serves 4
Cooking time 10–15 mins
Use Blender *or* Food Processor

1 large onion
2 cloves garlic
1 tablespoon oil
396 g (14 oz) can tomatoes (plus liquid from the can)
1 tablespoon Worcestershire sauce
few drops Tabasco sauce
1 teaspoon made mustard
salt and pepper

1 Peel and quarter the onion. Peel the garlic.
2 Heat the oil, add the onion and garlic and fry for several minutes. Add the rest of the ingredients and simmer for 10–15 minutes until a thick purée.

B OR **FP** 3   Tip the sauce into the warmed blender goblet or bowl of the food processor, using the double-bladed cutting knife. Fix the lid and switch on for a few seconds until a smooth sauce. Reheat if necessary.

To freeze
This sauce freezes well for 6 months.

To vary
Use 350 g (12 oz) fresh tomatoes, plus 4 tablespoons water.

HERB SAUCE Blend or process 300 ml ($\frac{1}{2}$ pt) low calorie natural yogurt with enough fresh chives, parsley, sage and tarragon (or other fresh herbs) to give 2 tablespoons. Flavour with a little mustard, lemon juice, salt and pepper.

Sweet sauces

When cooking fruit such as apples, peel, quarter and slice through the slicing attachment of a mixer or slicing disc of a food processor. Thin slices cook in a very few minutes and therefore retain more colour and flavour.

APPLE SAUCE Cook the sliced apples with 2–3 tablespoons only of water and sugar to taste, until just tender. A small knob of butter gives a pleasant flavour and shine. Tip into the warmed blender goblet or bowl of the food processor, fix the lid and switch on for a few seconds until smooth. Serve hot or cold with pork, duck or steamed puddings.

COOKED CRANBERRY SAUCE Put 450 g (1 lb) cranberries, 4 tablespoons water, 175 g (6 oz) sugar and 5 tablespoons water or 3–4 tablespoons water and 1–2 tablespoons port wine into a saucepan. Cover tightly and cook for 5–6 minutes. Tip into the warmed blender goblet or bowl of the food processor as in Apple Sauce above. Serve cold with turkey or with ice cream.

MELBA SAUCE Blend 1 level teaspoon arrowroot with 6 tablespoons water, 4 good tablespoons redcurrant jelly, 350 g (12 oz) raspberries, 50 g (2 oz) sugar. Stir over a

low heat until thickened. Cool, then either put through the sieve and colander attachment of the mixer to get rid of the pips, or use a blender or food processor, using the double-bladed cutting knife, and make a slightly less smooth sauce. Serve cold over ice cream and fruit.

ZABAGLIONE Although this can be served by itself Zabaglione makes a delicious accompaniment to fruit. The method of making this is very similar to that used in Hollandaise Sauce, see stage 2 on page 71. You must use a mixer and cannot make the sauce in a blender or food processor.

Put the yolks of 3 eggs into a bowl and add 50–75 g (2–3 oz) caster sugar. Whisk over hot water until thick and creamy. Slowly whisk in 3 tablespoons Marsala or Madeira. Serve warm.

Making Cream

Cream is one of the most usual sauces with fruit, the method of making and of whipping fresh cream follows.

You can make a good cream in the cream maker attachment of the mixer, the blender or the food processor using the double-bladed cutting knife. Use unsalted butter, taking care to heat it very gently. Accurate metric measures are given.

To calculate the amount of cream you will produce add together the weight of milk and butter used. A little mixture may be wasted in the saucepan, and in the appliance used.

In each case you need 110 ml (4 fl oz) milk.

For a *thin pouring cream* (like single cream) add 85 g (3 oz) unsalted butter.

For a *thick cream* (like double cream, but often not quite thick enough for whipping) add 110 g (4 oz) unsalted butter.

For a *very thick cream* (suitable for whipping) add 140 g (5 oz) unsalted butter.

1   Cut the butter into pieces, put into a saucepan with the milk and bring to blood heat, leave until the butter melts. Do not allow the milk to boil.

MA 2   Fix the cream maker of the mixer and pump the milk mixture through this.

B OR **FP**   Make sure the blender or food

processor bowl and double-bladed cutting knife are completely dry. Pour in the mixture. Fix the lid and switch on until smooth. You need an average total of 30 seconds in a blender i.e. three periods of 10 seconds, or 20 seconds in a food processor i.e. five periods of 4 seconds. Use the pulse if available in the food processor.

3   Put the cream into a container, cover and leave in the refrigerator for at least 2 hours, stir once or twice. Whip the thickest cream. Use in place of fresh cream.

To freeze
This is better freshly made.

WHIPPING CREAM You cannot whip double or whipping cream in a blender or food processor. Use a mixer on low speed and never over-whip.

Preparing stuffings

You need to make the stuffing in batches when using a blender, but the time taken is so short that this is not a great inconvenience. In the food processor however you can accommodate a greater quantity of ingredients.

PARSLEY AND THYME STUFFING

This stuffing is served with chicken, turkey, veal, fish or most savoury dishes.

Serves 4
Cooking time as the meat, poultry or fish, or 35 mins
Use Blender *or* Food Processor

100 g (4 oz) bread (weight without crusts)
50 g (2 oz) butcher's suet
enough parsley to give 2–3 tablespoons
**   when chopped**
enough thyme to give about 1 teaspoon
**   when chopped**
½ lemon
salt and pepper
1 egg

1   Break or cut the bread and suet into pieces. Sprig the parsley and remove the thyme leaves.
2   Pare the top rind (the 'zest') from the lemon and squeeze out the juice (as such a small amount is needed you can do this with a hand lemon squeezer).

B 3   Put a little bread, suet, lemon rind, parsley and thyme into the blender goblet. Switch to medium then high speed until all the ingredients are finely chopped. If your blender can take a larger amount feed more ingredients gradually through the cap in the centre of the lid with the machine in operation. Page 11 shows how to cut foil to fit the top of the goblet if the model does not have a removable cap.

FP   Place the double-bladed cutting knife and bowl in position. Add all the bread, suet, lemon rind and herbs, fix the lid and switch on until the ingredients are finely chopped; leave in the bowl.

B 4   Tip the prepared mixture into a mixing bowl, continue as stage 3 until all the ingredients are chopped, then add the lemon juice, salt, pepper and egg. Bind the stuffing together.

FP   Add salt, pepper, lemon juice and egg to the other ingredients in the bowl and switch on only long enough to bind the stuffing; do not over-process.

5   Cook the stuffing with the meat or other food or bake in a separate covered container in the centre of a moderately hot oven, 190–200°C, 375–400°F, Gas Mark 5–6, for 35 minutes. As the stuffing tends to dry out a little more when baked alone, add 1–2 tablespoons stock, milk or single cream if liked.

To freeze
The dry ingredients or mixed stuffing freezes well for 3 months.

To vary
Increase or vary the herbs – use fresh chives, tarragon, fennel or sage.
   Use packet suet, butter or margarine instead of butcher's suet. Melt the fat if using a blender. Allow to soften slightly if using a food processor. Add with the egg.

CELERY AND HERB STUFFING Add 2 or 3 chopped sticks from the celery heart.
   Excellent with fish.

CORN AND HERB STUFFING Add 75 g

(3 oz) well drained canned or cooked sweetcorn kernels.

Delicious with poultry.

LIVER AND HERB STUFFING Chop cooked calf's, lamb's or poultry liver with the bread, etc.

Excellent with poultry or veal.

MUSHROOM AND HERB STUFFING Chop 50 g (2 oz) raw mushrooms with the bread, etc.

This blends well with all foods.

ONION AND HERB STUFFING Chop 2 peeled medium raw or cooked onions with the bread, etc.

Use this stuffing with veal.

TOMATO AND HERB STUFFING Omit the egg and bind with 2 large skinned tomatoes, puréed after preparing the dry ingredients.

Particularly good with oily fish.

APRICOT STUFFING

This is good with lamb or chicken.

Serves 6–8
Cooking time as the meat or poultry, or 1 hour
Use Blender or Food Processor

100 g (4 oz) dried apricots
1 small onion
100 g (4 oz) bread (weight without crusts)
enough thyme to give 1 teaspoon
**   when chopped**
25 g (1 oz) butter
salt and pepper
1 tablespoon clear honey
1 egg

1   Halve each apricot if you want large pieces; for finely chopped apricots use the mincer attachment of a mixer or the food processor, see stage 3. Peel and quarter the onion.

2   Chop the bread, thyme and onion as described in stage 3 of Sage and Onion Stuffing on page 78.

3   Tip the bread, thyme and onion on to the apricots in a bowl. Melt the butter, add this and the rest of the ingredients to the apricot mixture; stir to bind. Soften the butter, add to the bread,

thyme and onion together with the salt, pepper, honey and egg. Fix the lid and switch on for a few seconds only to bind the ingredients. Keep the machine running and drop in the halved apricots through the feed-tube. Allow 1–2 seconds only if you want to keep the fruit in large pieces, but about 10 seconds if you prefer it finely chopped.

4   The stuffing is then ready to use. If baking in a separate container, cover to prevent the mixture hardening on top. Bake in the centre of a moderate oven, 160–180°C, 325–350°F, Gas Mark 3–4, for at least 1 hour (to make sure the apricots are tenderized).

To freeze
The dry ingredients or mixed stuffing freezes well for 3 months.

MUSHROOM STUFFING

This stuffing is excellent with many meats, but particularly with veal.

Serves 6–8
Cooking time as the meat, or 30 mins
Use Slicing Attachment of Mixer or Slicing Disc of Food Processor

175 g (6 oz) mushrooms
225 g (8 oz) sausagemeat
1 egg
salt and pepper

1   Wash or wipe the mushrooms with damp absorbent paper but do not peel them as the skin gives a great deal of flavour. Cut away just a very thin slice from the base of each stalk, but do not remove the stalk.

2   Fix the slicing attachment to the mixer or slicing disc to the food processor. If you have a choice select the one that gives the thinnest slices. Push the mushrooms through with the pusher.

3   Blend the sliced mushrooms with the sausagemeat and egg. Add a little salt and pepper.

4   The stuffing is then ready to use. If baking in a separate container, cover to prevent the mixture hardening on top. Bake in the centre of a moderately hot oven, 190°C, 375°F, Gas Mark 5, for 30 minutes.

To freeze
This stuffing freezes well for up to 6 months.

To vary

MUSHROOM AND TOMATO STUFFING
Slice 100 g (4 oz) mushrooms as before, blend with 100 g (4 oz) soft white or wholemeal breadcrumbs, 3 large skinned and coarsely chopped tomatoes, 2 tablespoons chopped parsley, 1 egg, 50 g (2 oz) melted butter, salt and pepper to taste.

This recipe is ideal for fish as well as poultry and meat.

MUSHROOM, CHEESE AND TOMATO STUFFING Follow the variation above but add 100 g (4 oz) grated cheese.

This is excellent with fish.

SAGE AND ONION STUFFING

Serve with pork, duck or goose; or with chicken instead of Parsley and Thyme Stuffing.
Serves 4
Cooking time as the meat or poultry, or 40–45 mins
Use Slicing Attachment of Mixer and Blender *or* use just the Blender (see stage 4) *or* Slicing Disc of Food Processor *or* use just Food Processor (see stage 4)

2 large onions
50–75 g (2–3 oz) bread (weight without crusts)
enough sage to give 1–2 teaspoons when chopped
salt and pepper
25–40 g (1–1½ oz) butcher's suet
1 egg

1   Peel the onions. Dice the bread. Wash the sage and pull the leaves from the stalks. There are two ways of making this stuffing. The onions may be semi-cooked, then chopped with the other ingredients; this gives a bland flavour, (see stages 2 and 3). Or the raw onions can be chopped with the ingredients, see stage 4, this gives a stronger taste and less smooth stuffing.

(MA or FP) 2   Before cooking the onions press through the slicing attachment of the mixer or slicing disc of the food processor. Put into a saucepan with a little water, salt and pepper, and simmer for 3–5 minutes; strain. Some liquid can be retained and used at stage 3.

(B) 3   Put the bread, suet and sage into the blender goblet, chop finely and tip into a mixing bowl. Finally chop the semi-cooked onions in the blender goblet for 1–2 seconds, add to the bread and sage,

mix with the egg, salt and pepper. Add a little onion stock for a more moist stuffing.

(FP)   Place the double-bladed cutting knife and bowl in position. Add the bread, suet and sage, fix the lid and switch on for a few seconds until almost chopped. Add the semi-cooked onions, egg, salt and pepper, process for a few seconds. Add a little onion stock for a more moist stuffing.

4   Quarter the uncooked onions.
(B)   Chop the onions with the bread, suet and sage. Transfer to a mixing bowl, add a little salt and pepper and the egg.
(FP)   Process the onions with the bread, suet and sage, until all the ingredients are chopped. Add the egg, a little salt and pepper, switch on to blend for 2 seconds.

5   As stage 5 under Parsley and Thyme Stuffing, page 76 but allow 40 minutes cooking time.

To freeze
This stuffing freezes well for 3 months.

To vary
CHESTNUT SAGE STUFFING Omit the breadcrumbs; blend the ingredients with 175 g (6 oz) unsweetened chestnut purée.
Excellent with pork.

SAUSAGE SAGE STUFFING Prepare the ingredients as stages 1, 2 and 3 above, blend with 225 g (8 oz) sausagemeat.
Serve with poultry.
Note: If you do not possess a blender or food processor, you can mince the bread and sage using the mincer attachment of a mixer, then mince the partially cooked or raw onions.

Stuffings for slimmers
A stuffing makes meat, or other food, more interesting and helps to keep it moist during cooking. You can substitute low calorie bread for ordinary bread in any recipe. Vegetables, particularly mushrooms, make good stuffings.

MUSHROOM STUFFING Put 1 peeled large onion, ½ green pepper, 100 g (4 oz) mushrooms through the slicing attachment of a mixer or slicing disc of a food processor. Blend with chopped parsley and 2–3 skinned and chopped tomatoes, add salt and pepper to taste. Excellent with fish, meat or poultry.

CHAPTER 9

VEGETABLES AND SALADS

Throughout this book you will find dishes using vegetables with details of the method of preparation for the particular recipe. The various types of mixers have taken away the tiresome and time-consuming job of chopping, grating or slicing vegetables. Here you will find a summary of the various ways in which you can cut vegetables for inclusion in cooked dishes or raw salads together with recipes.

Vegetables are peeled if necessary. Tomatoes are too soft to be put through a grater or slicer.

Ways to prepare vegetables

To chop vegetables
This gives a less even appearance to the vegetables than when grated or sliced, but it is satisfactory for most dishes.

IN A BLENDER
a) Cut the vegetables into 2·5–3·5-cm (1–1½-in) pieces. Put a small quantity into the blender goblet, fix the lid and switch on for a short time until chopped.
b) With hard vegetables such as carrots etc. you will achieve a better result if you drop pieces of the vegetable through the 'hole' in the lid – made by removing the cap or by making a foil lid or funnel, see page 11 – with the machine in operation.
c) Another way of chopping vegetables in the blender is to put them into the goblet with water or other liquid to cover. Switch on until chopped. The liquid can be discarded if not required.

IN A FOOD PROCESSOR
a) Cut the vegetables in 2·5–3·5-cm (1–1½-in) pieces. Place the double-bladed cutting knife and bowl in position. Add the vegetables, fix the lid and switch on for a few seconds. This method is ideal for onions, mushrooms and vegetables that are not too hard.
b) Hard vegetables such as carrots may be more satisfactorily chopped if pieces of the vegetable are dropped through the feed-tube with the machine in operation.

HERB BUTTER It is possible to chop fresh herbs in the food processor, as above, and blend them into butter in the bowl at the same time. Use Herb Butter for sandwiches or to garnish grilled meats and fish.

To grate and slice vegetables
Use the special attachments of the mixer or discs of a food processor. Manufacturers vary in the number they supply but food processors generally have a minimum of two.

IN A FOOD PROCESSOR
a) A grating disc, which you may find described as a shredding or chopping disc. Carrots and similar vegetables are grated neatly, and cucumber and softer vegetables are cut into tiny shreds.
b) A slicing disc produces neatly sliced cucumber, carrots, mushrooms, as well as shredded cabbage for Coleslaw and neatly shredded lettuce, etc.

If you want thicker and more 'chunky' pieces of vegetable you can use the disc which makes potato chips, available with many food processors.

Vegetable dishes

RUSSIAN CABBAGE Peel and slice 2 medium onions and 2 dessert apples. Fry in 50 g (2 oz) butter or margarine until soft. Meanwhile slice a red or green cabbage and cook in boiling salted water until just tender. Strain and reheat with the onions and apples. Serves 4–6

RATATOUILLE Peel 3 medium onions and 2–3 cloves garlic. Wash and trim 5–6 medium courgettes and 2 large aubergines. Put the vegetables through the shredding attachment of the mixer or shredding disc of the food processor – choose the attachment that gives the thinnest slices for the onions, but thicker slices for the courgettes and aubergines. Crush the garlic. Slice 675 g (1½ lb) tomatoes with a sharp knife. In the blender or food processor chop enough parsley to give 3–4 tablespoons.

Heat 4 tablespoons olive oil, add the onions, garlic and tomatoes and cook slowly for about 10 minutes. Add the courgettes and aubergines with salt and pepper to taste. Cover the pan and simmer gently for about 25–35 minutes or until vegetables are tender, but unbroken (these evenly sliced vegetables soften easily). Add half the parsley. Serve hot or cold, topped with the remaining parsley. Serves 6

PAN HAGGERTY Peel and slice enough potatoes to give 450 g (1 lb) and onions to give 225 g (8 oz), then slice 100 g (4 oz) Cheddar cheese.

Heat 50 g (2 oz) fat in a large frying pan. Put in a layer of potatoes, then a layer of onions and cheese. Continue the layers, seasoning between each, finishing with potatoes. Cover the frying pan with a lid or strong plate and cook gently for 15 minutes or until tender. Serves 4–6

POTATOES ANNA Peel 450 g (1 lb) potatoes and slice as thinly as possible. Brush a 18-cm (7-in) cake tin with melted fat. Arrange the potato slices neatly in the tin, brushing each layer with melted fat and seasoning. Bake in the centre of a moderate oven, 180°C, 350°F, Gas Mark 4, for 1¼ hours. Turn out and serve sliced like a cake. Serves 4

Everyone appreciates home-made cakes whether a simple sponge or something more elaborate Kraemmerhuse (page 88), Danish Easter Cake (page 88).

Salads

The ability to grate and slice raw vegetables finely means that many vegetables can be included in salads. Try sliced raw courgettes, grated raw beetroot and both red and green cabbage as well as the usual ingredients.

COLESLAW Slice cabbage as thinly as possible. Mix with mayonnaise, grated raw carrots, chopped nuts and/or celery.

MUSHROOM SALAD Slice button mushrooms. Mix with natural yogurt, a little oil and vinegar, chopped chives and chopped parsley. Season well.

CUCUMBER SALAD Grate or slice cucumber. Mix with natural yogurt and a little lemon juice, salt and pepper.

To mash vegetables
Cook and strain the vegetables.

IN A MIXER
If you have a portable mixer the vegetables may be mashed in the saucepan in which they were cooked. Break the cooked vegetables roughly with a fork, then beat with the mixer set to the lowest speed. When the vegetables are quite smooth, gradually whisk in butter or margarine and hot milk.

If using a larger mixer, tip the cooked vegetables into the mixing bowl, use the beater attachment and beat at a medium speed until smooth, then gradually beat in butter or margarine and hot milk.

IN A FOOD PROCESSOR
Some food processors have a plastic blade, in addition to the metal double-bladed cutting knife, and this could be used for mashing potatoes. If not available, use the metal knife. Dice or slice the cooked vegetables. Place the plastic or metal cutting knife and bowl in position. Add the vegetables with a little butter or margarine and hot milk. Fix the lid, switch on and blend for a few seconds. Do not over-beat.

POTATO CROQUETTES Mash potatoes as above, adding butter or margarine but no milk. Allow the mixture to cool, form into finger shapes, coat in seasoned flour, then beaten egg. Roll in crisp breadcrumbs. Heat deep fat or oil to 170°C, 338°F, and deep fry the croquettes until crisp and golden. Drain on absorbent paper.

CHAPTER 10

DESSERTS AND CAKES

One of the ways in which you will derive great pleasure in menu planning is the ease with which you can produce deliciously light desserts based on fruit purées, using a blender or food processor. They are invaluable for this purpose.

The mixer or food processor also will enable you to mix pastry in record time, so that pies and tarts become incredibly quick and simple to make.

New users of mixers are always worried whether they have to use completely different recipes for their favourite cakes, biscuits and sponge puddings. There is no need. All recipes can be produced with the mixer, but you need to appreciate the effect of the vigorous action. This is even more important with a food processor; there are some cakes which cannot be prepared with this appliance. You will find advice on the various types of mixtures on pages 85 to 89.

Using fruit purées

While hard fruits such as plums, firm gooseberries etc. need to be cooked in a little water, soft fruits such as raspberries can be made into a purée without cooking. Sweeten the fruit to taste.

A thick fruit purée means using little, if any water, with the fruit. A thin purée means using enough water to give a pouring consistency.

There are three ways to turn fruit into a purée:

a) Rub through the sieve and colander attachment of the mixer. All pips, skin and stones are left behind.

b) In the blender.

c) In the food processor, using the double-bladed cutting knife.

Stones must be removed before using a blender or food processor. As all the pips and skin are not completely puréed, you may prefer to use a hand sieve afterwards; this will be easy to use as the fruit is already puréed.

These desserts give 3–4 small portions.

FRUIT FOULE (FOOL) Make 300 ml ($\frac{1}{2}$ pt) *very thick* sweetened purée. Put into the blender goblet or bowl of the food processor with 300 ml ($\frac{1}{2}$ pt) thick sweetened custard. Switch on for a few seconds until the mixture is velvet-like. Spoon into glasses and chill. Top with cream.

FRUIT MOUSSE Make 300 ml ($\frac{1}{2}$ pt) thick sweetened fruit purée. Sprinkle 2 teaspoons gelatine on to 2 tablespoons water or fruit juice in a small bowl. Stand the bowl over hot water until the gelatine has dissolved. Blend the gelatine into the purée; allow to stiffen slightly, then fold in 150 ml ($\frac{1}{4}$ pt) whipped cream and finally 2 stiffly whisked egg whites. Spoon into glasses. When set, top with whipped cream.

FRUIT SOUFFLÉ Make 200 ml ($7\frac{1}{2}$ fl oz) thick unsweetened fruit purée. Blend with 1 tablespoon cornflour. Put into a saucepan, add 50 g (2 oz) sugar and 25 g (1 oz) butter, and stir over a low heat until thickened. Separate 3 eggs, beat the yolks into the fruit mixture, then fold in the stiffly whisked egg whites. Spoon into a 15–18-cm (6–7-in) buttered soufflé dish. Bake in the centre of a moderately hot oven, 190°C, 375°F, Gas Mark 5, for 30–35 minutes. Dust with icing sugar and serve at once.

RØDGRØD Make 600 ml (1 pt) absolutely smooth thin fruit purée (raspberries with redcurrants is an ideal mixture). Blend with 1 tablespoon cornflour and pour into a saucepan. Stir well over a low heat until thickened; add sugar to taste. Spoon into glasses and leave until cold. Top with chopped nuts and serve with cream.

FRUIT SORBET Make 600 ml (1 pt) thin fruit purée, sweeten to taste but keeping a fairly sharp taste. Dissolve 1 teaspoon gelatine in 2 tablespoons water or fruit juice, see Fruit Mousse, and add to the purée. Freeze lightly, then fold in 2 stiffly whisked egg whites. Return to the freezer. Remove from the freezer a short while before serving to soften a little.

Rich flans

Flan pastry is often called biscuit crust pastry as it is rather similar in texture to a biscuit in that it is sweet and very crisp, see page 84. The following recipe gives another rich pastry-like crust.

LINZERTORTE

Read the information about pastry on page 84; this rich dough must not be over-handled.

Serves 6–8
Cooking time 35–40 mins
Use Mixer *or* Food Processor

½ lemon (rind only)
85 g* (3 oz) unsalted butter
85 g* (3 oz) plain flour
½ teaspoon ground cinnamon
85 g* (3 oz) caster sugar
85 g* (3 oz) ground almonds
2 egg yolks
¼ teaspoon vanilla essence
350 g (12 oz) thick raspberry jam
To glaze
1 egg yolk
1 tablespoon cream or milk
*Use this metrication

1 Finely grate the lemon rind with a hand grater. Cut the butter into pieces.
M 2 Fix the beater or whisk(s). Put the flour, cinnamon, sugar, ground almonds, lemon rind and butter into the mixer. Switch to low speed only until the mixture resembles fine breadcrumbs.
FP Place the double-bladed cutting knife and bowl in position. Add the flour, cinnamon, sugar, ground almonds, lemon rind and butter. Fix the lid, switch on for a few seconds only until the mixture resembles fine breadcrumbs.

3 Beat the egg yolks and add the vanilla essence. Add to the rubbed in mixture.
M 4 Switch to low speed only until a soft dough.
FP Fix the lid and switch on for 2–3 seconds only until a soft dough.
5 Wrap the dough and chill for 1 hour. Grease a 24-cm (9½-in) flan dish.
6 Knead the dough lightly on a floured surface. Reserve just under a quarter of the dough for the lattice strips.
7 Press the remaining dough over the base and up sides of the dish and spread the jam evenly over the base of the flan.
8 Roll out the reserved dough on a well floured surface to a rectangle 20×7·5 cm (8×3 in); cut into 6 strips.
9 Lift the strips carefully, lay them across the jam in a lattice pattern.
10 Loosen the top pastry edges with a knife; fold towards the jam to make a 1-cm (½-in) border. Beat the egg yolk and cream or milk, and use to brush over the pastry. Chill for 30 minutes. Bake in the centre of a moderate oven, 180°C, 350°F, Gas Mark 4, for 35–40 minutes or until crisp and lightly browned. Serve cold.

Making ice creams

Many ice cream recipes recommend aerating the mixture by beating after it has been lightly frozen.

M 1 Whip 300 ml (½ pt) double cream until it just holds its shape; do not overwhip. (This cannot be done in a food processor.) For a lighter ice cream, use half double and half single cream.
2 Whisk in 25–50 g (1–2 oz) sifted icing or caster sugar. Transfer to a freezing tray and freeze until just firm.
M 3 Return the mixture to the mixer bowl and whisk until fluffy.
FP Place either the plastic knife or the double-bladed cutting knife and bowl in position. Fix the lid and switch on until light and fluffy.
Return to the freezer.

Flavourings
CHOCOLATE Blend in 2 tablespoons chocolate powder at stage 2.

COFFEE Blend 3 level teaspoons instant coffee powder with 1 tablespoon hot water, cool and add to the cream at stage 2.

COFFEE AND GINGER (*Illustrated on page 72*) Chop 3–4 pieces of stem ginger and add to the coffee ice cream at the end of stage 3.

You can add well drained diced canned apricots or raisins instead of ginger.

FRUIT Use double cream and up to 200 ml (7½ fl oz) thick fruit purée.

Making batters

A pancake batter is not particularly troublesome to make by hand, but you are sure of a smooth mixture with little effort if you use a mixer, blender or food processor.

Batters using the mixer
Put the flour and salt into the mixing bowl, add the egg(s) and a few tablespoons of the liquid. Whisk the ingredients together at the slowest speed, this will prevent the flour flying, then gradually whisk in the remaining liquid.

Batters using the blender
Pour the liquid and break the egg(s) into the blender goblet, then add the flour and salt. This prevents flour adhering to the inside of the blender goblet and not being completely blended. Put on the lid, switch to the lowest speed to prevent the mixture splashing, then use a higher speed and blend until a smooth batter. The mixture is well aerated and there will be a layer of bubbles on top; allow these to subside before using the batter.

Batters using the food processor
Place either the double-bladed cutting knife or the plastic knife and bowl in position. To avoid undue splashing, pour about a third of the liquid into the bowl. Add the egg(s), then the flour and salt. Fix the lid and switch on for a few seconds; with the machine in operation, pour the remaining liquid gradually through the feed-tube. Process until a smooth batter. *Note*: Sifting flour is unnecessary with such efficient mixing.

PANCAKES Use 110 g* (4 oz) plain flour, pinch salt, 1 egg and 300 ml (½ pt) milk or milk and water, or use 2 eggs (then deduct 2 tablespoons liquid from the 300 ml (½ pt)). Make the batter using one of the described methods.
*Use this metrication
Heat a very little fat or oil in a pan; pour in enough batter to give a paper-thin layer. Cook for 1–2 minutes then toss or turn and cook on the second side. Fill with fruit purée, jam or serve with sugar and lemon. Makes about 12 pancakes

Making pastry

Shortcrust and flan pastry can be prepared in a mixer or food processor with great success. Never try and make too much pastry at one time, follow the manufacturer's advice as to quantities.

NEVER over-mix or over-process pastry or it will be difficult to handle.

Pastry using the mixer
Sift the flour and pinch of salt into the dry bowl. Cut the fat into 2.5–3.5-cm (1–1½-in) pieces and add to the flour.

If using a hand mixer – switch on and move the whisk gently through the mixture until it resembles fine breadcrumbs. Add the liquid gradually and switch on again to blend the ingredients.

Manufacturers of large mixers suggest you select the beater attachment. I find I can use the whisk too, for small amounts of pastry. Follow the advice above and add the liquid gradually with the machine in operation using the lowest speed.

Pastry using the food processor
It is important to appreciate the speed with which the flour and fat are processed. Place the double-bladed cutting knife and bowl in position. Sift the flour into the bowl. Cut the fat in small pieces, as described above, and add to the flour. Fix the lid and switch on for a few seconds. Add the liquid very gradually through the feed-tube; the dough will form a ball around the knife. *Note:* Because of the vigorous action of a mixer or food processor you will find you can cut down from 110 g* (4 oz) to 85 g* (3 oz) fat to 225 g (8 oz) flour and still have good pastry. You will use a little less liquid than when mixing pastry by hand.

SHORTCRUST PASTRY Use 225 g (8 oz) plain flour, pinch salt, 85–110 g* (3–4 oz) fat and water to mix.
*Use this metrication

To vary
Add a little pepper and mustard to the flour for savoury pastry.
    Add 25 g (1 oz) caster sugar to the flour for sweet shortcrust.

FRUIT CRUMBLE
Serves 4–6
Cooking time 30–45 mins
Use Mixer *or* Food Processor

For the crumble
175 g (6 oz) self-raising or plain flour
85 g* (3 oz) butter or margarine
85–110 g* (3–4 oz) granulated or
   Demerara or caster sugar

450–550 g (1–1¼ lb) fruit (weight when
   prepared)
water (see method)
sugar to taste
*Use this metrication

1   Read about pastry opposite.
M
OR 2   Put the flour into the mixer or bowl of
FP   the food processor; cut the fat into
        pieces and add to the flour.
M 3   Add the sugar, switch on to a low speed
        until like fine breadcrumbs.
FP   Fix the lid and switch on until like fine
        breadcrumbs. Add the sugar and
        process for 1–2 seconds. The food
        processor grinds sugar finely and the
        gritty texture of sugar grains improves a
        crumble.
    4   Prepare the fruit and put into a pie dish.
        Add a very little water to hard fruit,
        such as apples, with sugar to taste;
        cover and cook in a moderate oven,
        180°C, 350°F, Gas Mark 4, for about 10
        minutes. Soft fruit will not require water
        or pre-cooking.
    5   Sprinkle the crumble mixture over the
        fruit and flatten gently with a knife.
    6   Bake in the centre of a moderate oven,
        160–180°C, 325–350°F, Gas Mark 3–4, for
        30–35 minutes.
To freeze
Freeze before or after cooking for up to 3 months.
To vary
SPICED CRUMBLE Add spice or nutmeg or cinnamon to the flour.
NUT CRUMBLE Add 50 g (2 oz) chopped nuts to the flour or drop the nuts into the flour mixture when almost mixed.

Making cakes by the rubbing-in method

The information given on the previous page for pastry applies when making cakes by this method. Remember:
a) If you add dried fruit, as in Rock Buns, you must add the fruit at the very last moment when using a food processor, otherwise it will be chopped so finely that it just disappears into the mixture.
b) Do not over-handle.
c) You may need a little less liquid than when mixing by hand.

ROCK BUNS Self-raising flour does not need sifting in this type of recipe, but sift plain flour and baking powder.
M   Place the beater or whisk(s) of the mixer
OR or double-bladed cutting knife and bowl of
FP the food processor in position. Cut 110 g*
    (4 oz) butter or margarine into pieces; if
    hard leave for a while to soften. This is not
    necessary with luxury soft margarine.
        Put 225 g (8 oz) self-raising flour, or sift
    plain flour and 2 teaspoons baking powder,
    into the mixer or bowl of the processor.
    Add the butter or margarine with 110 g*
    (4 oz) caster or granulated sugar. Fix the lid
    of the processor and switch on until the
    mixture resembles fine breadcrumbs.
M   Add 75–100 g (3–4 oz) dried fruit and
    1 egg. Blend on a low speed, then continue
    mixing while adding enough milk to make
    a sticky consistency, i.e. the mixture should
    easily be pulled into peaks.
FP Add 1 egg, fix the lid and process for 1–2
    seconds only. With the machine in
    operation, add the milk slowly through the
    feed-tube until a sticky consistency. Add
    75–100 g (3–4 oz) dried fruit and switch on
    for 1–2 seconds only.
        Grease 2 baking trays, spoon about
    12 mounds of mixture on to the trays and
    sprinkle with a little sugar. Bake towards
    the top of a moderately hot to hot oven,
    200–220°C, 400–425°F, Gas Mark 6–7, for
    about 12 minutes. Cool for 2–3 minutes
    before removing from the trays.
*Use this metrication

Making cakes by the creaming method

IN A MIXER

Both smaller hand mixers and the larger mixers are suitable for combining fat and sugar in the 'creaming' process. The amount that can be creamed together depends upon the size and motor capacity of the mixer. It is unsatisfactory to make the mixer deal with an excessive quantity, so check the manufacturer's instructions.

a) Modern luxury (soft-type) margarines soften easily, but if the butter or margarine is hard either warm the mixing bowl before adding the fat or cut it into pieces and leave at room temperature to soften. Do NOT melt it, for one purpose of creaming is to incorporate the maximum amount of air and so soften and lighten the mixture.

b) Use the lowest speed at the beginning of the creaming action, then increase slightly if necessary; do not use maximum speed.

c) Add the eggs gradually to prevent the fat mixture curdling.

d) Fold in the flour, or flour and baking powder, with a metal spoon or use the lowest speed for the minimum period. Sifting the flour is an advantage for these cakes.

IN A FOOD PROCESSOR

The food processor does not aerate the mixture in the same way as a mixer. The best results are achieved by using luxury or softened butter or margarine, then putting all the ingredients for the cake into the processor bowl with the double-bladed cutting knife in position, and mixing together for a few seconds. It is important to follow the manufacturer's advice as to the maximum amount to mix at one time and not to over-process. If adding dried or glacé fruit to the mixture see the advice under Rock Buns on page 85.

CHERRY AND WALNUT UPSIDE DOWN PUDDING

Serves 6
Cooking time 50 mins
Use Blender and Mixer *or* Food Processor

For the topping
75 g (3 oz) glacé cherries
75 g (3 oz) walnuts
25 g (1 oz) butter
50 g (2 oz) soft brown sugar
1 tablespoon coffee essence
For the sponge base
110 g* (4 oz) butter
110 g* (4 oz) caster sugar
2 eggs
175 g (6 oz) self-raising flour or plain flour and 1½ teaspoons baking powder
2 tablespoons coffee essence
*Use this metrication

1　Grease an 18-cm (7-in) cake tin without a loose base or a soufflé dish. Quarter or coarsely chop the cherries with damp kitchen scissors.

B 2　Put the walnuts into the blender goblet and chop fairly coarsely.

FP　Place the double-bladed cutting knife and bowl in position. Add the walnuts, fix the lid and switch on for a few seconds only to chop the nuts.

3　Melt the butter and brown sugar for the topping, stir in the cherries, walnuts and coffee essence. Spread over the base of the tin or dish.

M 4　Warm the mixer bowl, select the beater if using a larger mixer. Cut the butter in pieces, put into the bowl with the sugar; cream until soft and light as described opposite. Gradually beat in the eggs.

M 5　Sift the flour or flour and baking powder into the creamed mixture; either fold in by hand, or with the mixer on the lowest speed. Fold in the coffee essence.

FP　Soften the butter at room temperature; sift the flour or flour and baking powder. Using the double-bladed cutting knife, put all the ingredients into the bowl; fix the lid and switch on for about 25 seconds.

6　Spoon the mixture over the cherry and walnut base and bake in the centre of a moderate oven, 180°C, 350°F, Gas Mark 4, for about 50 minutes or until firm to the touch.

7　Turn out on to a heated serving dish; serve hot with cream or ice cream.

To freeze
Freeze in the tin or dish; turn out and wrap. Use within 3 months.

VICTORIA SANDWICH

This very light sponge cake depends upon three factors for complete success.

1. You need a correct balance of ingredients.
2. It is essential to use the right method of handling the ingredients. If the creamed fat, sugar and egg mixture is allowed to curdle you will never obtain a perfect texture.

    If the flour is over-beaten into the creamed ingredients you will have a less light sponge.
3. Select the correct baking temperature and position in the oven. Ovens vary so two settings are suggested in the recipe below. Check with the recommendations given by the cooker manufacturer. Too high a temperature means the outside of the sponge is over-cooked before the centre, whereas too low a temperature means the sponge tends to dry more.

Read the advice given about mixtures made by the creaming method opposite.

To make two 15–16.5-cm (6–6½-in) sponges or one deeper cake use

110 g* (4 oz) butter or margarine
110 g* (4 oz) caster sugar
2 large eggs
110 g* (4 oz) self-raising flour or plain flour
  and 1 level teaspoon baking powder
  *Use this metrication

To make two 19–20-cm (7½–8-in) sponges or one deeper cake use

175 g (6 oz) butter or margarine
175 g (6 oz) caster sugar
3 large eggs
175 g (6 oz) self-raising flour or plain flour
  and 1½ level teaspoons baking powder

M 1 Fix the beater or whisks, depending upon mixer. Read the notes opposite about softening fat. Cream the butter or margarine and sugar on low speed, then gradually add the eggs and beat into the mixture, slowly and carefully.

M 2 Sift the flour, or flour and baking powder into the creamed mixture. Either fold in by hand or with the mixer on lowest speed. Switch off the mixer as soon as the flour is incorporated into the other ingredients.

FP Read the notes opposite about softening fat. Place the double-bladed cutting knife and bowl in position. Add all the ingredients, fix the lid and switch on for about 25 seconds.

3. Grease and flour or line the tin(s). Spoon in the mixture.
4. Bake the sandwich cakes just above the centre of a moderate oven, 180–190°C, 350–375°F, Gas Mark 4–5. Allow 15–20 minutes for the smaller sponges and 20–25 minutes for the larger ones.

    Bake the mixture in one tin in the centre of a moderate oven, 160°C, 325°F, Gas Mark 3 for 40 minutes for the smaller size and for 50 minutes for the larger size.
5. Test to see if cooked by pressing gently on top; if your finger leaves no impression the sponge is cooked.
6. Turn out carefully on to a wire rack and leave to cool. Sandwich together with jam and/or whipped cream or fruit. Dust the top with sieved icing, or caster, sugar.

Successful light cakes

The recipe opposite and the sponge below give an indication of the method to follow when making a light sponge cake by creaming in a mixer or food processor.

Use this technique for similar cakes using you own favourite recipes.

When you prepare rich fruit cakes be particularly careful that the mixture is not over-beaten or over-processed. Pay particular attention to timing when adding dried or glacé fruit to the mixture in a food processor. Allow 1–2 seconds processing time only, otherwise the fruit will be so finely chopped that it becomes a purée.

These cakes can be frozen for 3 months.

Based on a Victoria sandwich

There are many ways to incorporate flavour into the Victoria sandwich, i.e. cream the finely grated rind of a lemon or orange with the fat and sugar; substitute 1 tablespoon cocoa powder for 1 tablespoon flour in the smaller sponge or 1½ tablespoons in the larger quantity. Use small eggs and blend the ingredients together with very strong coffee.

When making these flavoured sponges, it is usual to fill and top the cake with a butter cream.

DANISH EASTER CAKE
(Illustrated on page 80)

Follow the recipe for making the Victoria Sandwich on page 87, using 110 g (4 oz) butter etc. When cold, sandwich and top with lemon butter cream, made by creaming 75 g (3 oz) softened unsalted butter with 175 g (6 oz) sieved icing sugar, the finely grated rind of 1 lemon and 2 teaspoons lemon juice.

Butter creams can also be flavoured with orange rind and juice, chocolate or cocoa powder, strong coffee etc.

Allow the butter to soften at room temperature before beating or processing.

MADEIRA CAKE Follow the method for the Victoria Sandwich on page 87, but use 175 g (6 oz) butter or margarine, 175 g (6 oz) caster sugar, 3 large eggs, 3 tablespoons milk and 225 g (8 oz) self-raising flour or plain flour and 2 teaspoons baking powder. Put into an 18-cm (7-in) greased and floured cake tin. Top with a sprinkling of caster sugar; add a thick slice of candied citron peel half way through the cooking time. Bake in the centre of a moderate oven, 160°C, 325°F, Gas Mark 3, for about 1¼ hours.

This cake can be adapted by adding 1–2 teaspoons ground ginger or other spices, or about 225 g (8 oz) currants or other dried fruit.

A Lemon or Orange cake is made by creaming the finely grated rind of 1 lemon or 2 oranges with the fat and sugar and mixing the cake with fruit juice instead of milk.

DUNDEE CAKE Follow the proportions for Madeira cake above, but omit 1 tablespoon milk and use half plain and half self-raising flour or add only 1 teaspoon baking powder to the plain flour. Add 450 g (1 lb) mixed dried fruit, 50 g (2 oz) chopped blanched almonds, 50 g (2 oz) chopped glacé cherries and 50 g (2 oz) chopped candied peel. Put into a 20-cm (8-in) greased and floured cake tin, top with blanched almonds and bake in the centre of a moderate oven, 160°C, 325°F, Gas Mark 3, for about 2 hours.

Making biscuits

In some biscuit recipes the fat is rubbed into the flour, in others the ingredients are creamed together. It also is possible to make biscuits by melting certain ingredients. Whichever method is given in a recipe, you will find the mixer or food processor is ideal for kneading the biscuit dough. The vigorous action combines the ingredients efficiently and quickly. You may well find that you must be a little more sparing in the amount of liquid used when mixing or processing the dough compared to mixing by hand.

The following is typical of a rich shortbread type biscuit in which no liquid is used. Store in an airtight tin.

SHORTBREAD CRISPS

M **or** **FP** 1 Place the beater or whisks of a mixer or double-bladed cutting knife of a food processor in position.

2 Put 75 g (3 oz) butter or margarine, 50 g (2 oz) caster sugar and 110 g* (4 oz) self-raising flour or plain flour and 1 teaspoon baking powder into the mixing bowl or bowl of the food processor.

M 3 Switch to the lowest speed until the ingredients blend together.

FP Fix the lid, switch on for about 20 seconds until the ingredients blend together.

4 Divide into 12–15 portions (chill for a short time if slightly sticky). Place on to 2 ungreased baking trays, allowing room to spread, and bake in the centre of a moderate oven, 160–180°C, 325–350°F, Gas Mark 3–4, for 15 minutes.

*Use this metrication

KRAEMMERHUSE

(Illustrated on page 80)

These Danish biscuit-like cakes show how you can combine electric and hand mixing. If you hate creaming mixtures by hand you could use the food processor, but you will probably find it easier to scrape the creamed mixture out of the processor bowl into the bowl in which you have whisked the egg whites; for folding is not easy in the processor bowl.

If using a hand mixer you can remove the whisks after creaming the butter and sugar; wash and dry these well, then use them to whisk the egg whites.

1 Save several clean, dry milk bottles, for you need these to help shape the cones. It is important in this recipe to preheat the oven; set to moderately hot, 200°C, 400°F, Gas Mark 6.

M 2 Put 125 g (4½ oz) butter and 125 g (4½ oz) caster sugar into the mixing bowl; beat together on low speed until a light fluffy mixture. Sift 110 g* (4 oz) plain flour into the bowl. Fold into the creamed mixture with a metal spoon or on low speed for the minimum period.

M 3 Whisk the whites of 4 large eggs until frothy in a bowl, fold into the creamed mixture with a metal spoon.

4 Grease at least 2 large baking trays. Using a teaspoon, place about 4 mounds of the mixture well apart on each tray allowing adequate space between for spreading. Keep the remaining mixture covered in the bowl until ready to use. Dip a palette knife in cold water, shake fairly dry and spread the mounds out into wafer-thin rounds.

5 Deal with one batch at a time. Bake for 5–6 minutes just above the centre of the oven or until the edges turn a delicate brown.

6 Quickly remove each biscuit from the baking tray with a damp palette knife and twist into a cone with your fingers. Place into the neck of a milk bottle to set then transfer to a wire tray.

7 Continue cooking the remainder of the mixture, greasing the baking trays as necessary.

8 Put into airtight tins as soon as cool. Whip the cream, fill each cone just before serving; decorate with a strawberry.
*Use this metrication

To freeze
The unfilled cones keep in an airtight tin; freezing is not necessary.

To vary
LANGUES DE CHAT Proceed to stage 4 as above; put the mixture into a large piping bag with a 0.5-cm (¼-in) plain piping nozzle. Pipe fingers of the mixture on to well greased baking trays. Bake as above.

MAKING SPONGES BY THE WHISKING METHOD

A food processor is not suitable for this method of mixing.

To make two 19–20-cm (7½–8-in) sponges or one deeper cake use

3 large eggs
110 g* (4 oz) caster sugar
85 g* (3 oz) self-raising flour or plain flour
   and ¾ level teaspoon baking powder
*Use this metrication

M 1 Fix the whisk(s). Break the eggs into the mixing bowl, add the sugar. Start on a lower speed then switch to high speed until you can see the trail of the whisk(s) in the mixture; it should be the consistency of thick cream.

2 Sift the flour or flour and baking powder twice, then fold into the whisked eggs and sugar with a metal spoon or palette knife.

3 Grease and flour the tin or tins. Put in the mixture.

4 Bake the sponge sandwiches above the centre of a moderate oven, 190°C, 375°F, Gas Mark 5, for about 12 minutes; bake the one large sponge cake in the centre of a moderate oven, 160–180°C, 325–350°F, Gas Mark 3–4, for about 35 minutes until firm to a gentle touch.

To freeze
This cake freezes exceptionally well for up to 3 months. Open freeze then wrap.

MERINGUES

The mixer is invaluable for whisking egg whites for all purposes, especially for meringues. Where there is a choice of a beater or whisking attachment on a large mixer, always use the whisk and select a high speed.

The food processor is not suitable for making meringues, even when the particular model has a double-bladed cutting knife designed to whisk egg whites. By stopping and starting the processor, or using the pulse, if the model has one, it is possible to blend sugar into the egg whites, but the result can be extremely disappointing.

Successful meringues
Take the eggs out of the refrigerator an hour or so before whisking the whites; cold egg whites will not whisk, neither will eggs *less* than 24 hours old.

M Make sure the mixer bowl is dry and free from any speck of fat, egg yolk, etc. Do not economize on sugar, as you will see from the recommended metric weight.

To each egg white allow 55 g* (2 oz) sugar. This can be all caster sugar or half caster and half seived icing sugar.
*Use this metrication

Quantities to allow

3 egg whites and 175 g (6 oz) sugar will give about 36 tiny meringues, 12 large shells, or 8–10 nests.

Whisk the egg whites until very stiff (but not so dry that they are crumbly) on high speed. There are various ways of adding the sugar:

a) Whisk in half the sugar on low speed, fold in the remainder by hand using a metal spoon.
b) Whisk in all the sugar gradually on low speed.
c) Fold in all the sugar by hand (this tends to give a softer mixture).

To make individual meringues

Oil a baking tray, or cover it with oiled greaseproof paper, or use silicone paper.

Put spoonfuls of the mixture on to the trays or put the meringue mixture into a piping bag with a 0.5-1-cm ($\frac{1}{4}$–$\frac{1}{2}$-in) plain or rose piping nozzle.

Bake for 1 hour for tiny meringues, up to 2$\frac{1}{2}$–3 hours for large ones, at the lowest setting in your oven, see under Pavlova. The meringues are adequately cooked when they come away from the tray easily. Cool and store in an airtight tin.

To freeze

Meringues never become really frozen due to the high sugar content. Freezing is really unnecessary, as they store well in an airtight tin.

To vary

VANILLA MERINGUES Add a few drops vanilla essence to the egg whites.
Other essences can also be used.

CHOCOLATE MERINGUES Allow 1–1$\frac{1}{2}$ teaspoons sieved cocoa powder or 2–3 teaspoons chocolate powder to each 55 g* (2 oz) sugar.

COFFEE MERINGUES Allow a scant 1 teaspoon instant coffee powder to each 55 g* (2 oz) sugar. Blend with the sugar.

MERINGUE NESTS Shape part of the meringue mixture into rounds; put the remaining mixture into the piping bag and pipe an edge, i.e. make miniature Pavlova shapes (8–10). When cold, fill as for Pavlova.

Do not put the whipped cream or ice cream into a meringue until just before serving. If left for too long, the filling tends to soften the crisp meringue.

PAVLOVA This name is given to a large meringue shape.

To make a good-sized Pavlova use 4 egg whites and 110 g* (4 oz) sugar. To encourage a crisp outside to the meringue, but a slightly sticky centre, mix 1 teaspoon cornflour with the sugar. Whisk the egg whites, with a few drops of vanilla essence, add the sugar as recommended under Meringues. Finally, fold in 1 teaspoon brown or white malt vinegar. Spoon or pipe the meringue into a flan shape on the prepared baking tray. Bake at the coolest temperature in your oven, i.e. 110–130°C, 225–250°F, Gas Mark $\frac{1}{4}$–$\frac{1}{2}$, for 2$\frac{1}{2}$–3 hours. When cool, fill with whipped cream or ice cream and fruit.

*Use this metrication.

To make icings and fillings

A small or large mixer can be used for all types of icings and fillings; a food processor can be used for some icings.

To give smooth icing sugar

Icing sugar tends to develop small, hard lumps if it is stored for any length of time. These lumps can be removed if the icing sugar is put into a blender goblet or the food processor.

Make quite certain that the goblet or bowl and cutting knife of the food processor are completely dry before adding the icing sugar. Blend or process for a few seconds until a smooth powder.

In an emergency you can grind granulated sugar so finely that it becomes powdered into icing sugar. The colour may not be quite as white as the icing sugar you buy, but that will not matter if you are tinting the icing or filling.

BUTTER CREAM

This mixture is ideal as a filling or topping for sponge and other cakes. A basic recipe is given on page 88 under the Danish Easter Cake. The proportions of butter and smooth icing sugar used can be varied. The more icing sugar used the firmer the icing becomes.

Keep the butter (or good quality margarine) at room temperature for a time before creaming with the sugar and flavouring.

Use the beater with a larger mixer and the double-bladed cutting knife of the food processor.

ROYAL ICING

There is a tendency to over-beat and over-aerate this icing. This can cause problems in coating the cake and in piping because over-beating produces tiny air bubbles. The golden rule, therefore, is to stop beating as soon as the icing is white and glossy. The basic proportions are 1 egg white, 225 g (8 oz) icing sugar, $\frac{1}{4}-\frac{1}{2}$ tablespoon lemon juice, and 1 teaspoon glycerine (to give a softer icing). Most small mixers can only cope with making icing using 450 g (1 lb) icing sugar at one time; most food processors can deal with up to 900 g (2 lb) icing sugar at one time.

M 1 Fix the beater of the large mixer or whisk(s) of the smaller models. Put the egg white(s) into the mixer bowl, whisk or beat for a few seconds only. Add the rest of the ingredients and blend on the lowest speed; switch to maximum speed only until shiny and smooth.

FP Place the double-bladed cutting knife and bowl in position. Add the egg white(s), fix the lid and switch on until frothy. Add the remaining ingredients and switch on for about 10 seconds.

2 Keep the icing covered with a damp cloth to prevent drying until ready to use.

GLACÉ ICING

This simple icing is ideal for sponges, cakes and biscuits. To 225 g (8 oz) smooth icing sugar you need approximately $\frac{3}{4}-1$ tablespoon hot or cold water, fruit juice or liquid coffee for a stiff consistency, $1\frac{1}{2}-2$ tablespoons liquid for a flowing consistency.

This icing is not suitable for piping, except for making a simple design or lettering using a writing nozzle.

M 1 Put the icing sugar into the mixer bowl, and gradually add enough liquid to bind. Stir with a spoon initially to prevent the light icing sugar flying in all directions. Fix the whisk(s) and whisk on a high speed until blended.

FP Place either the plastic knife or the double-bladed cutting knife and bowl in position. Add the icing sugar, fix the lid and switch on for a few seconds until the icing sugar is smooth. Pour the liquid through the feed-tube and continue processing for a few seconds.

2 Flavourings, such as a few drops of essence, can be added with the liquid. Use the icing as soon as it is blended.

Yeast recipes

The time-consuming job in yeast cookery is the thorough kneading of the dough. This is essential to distribute the yeast and therefore to produce a uniformly good texture in the bread or cake. The dough hook, available with larger mixers, is ideal for kneading any yeast dough. Check the manufacturer's instructions as to the maximum amount of dough to handle at one time.

It is possible to have two dough kneaders to fit in place of the whisks with some small mixers. Knead up to 0.5 kg (1 lb) flour etc. at one time.

Select the lowest speed with all mixers.

A food processor can be used for kneading but you must switch off after about 10 seconds to prevent over-handling.

Do not knead doughs with more than 0.5 kg (1 lb) flour etc. at one time.

The unusual recipe below includes important points to check, see stages 4, 5, 7, 8.

Kneaded dough test
To test if the dough is sufficiently kneaded before proving (as in stage 4 below), or after shaping, as stage 5 in the particular recipe on this page, press the dough firmly with a floured finger. If the impression of your finger is left in the dough then continue kneading. If the impression comes out, the dough is ready for the next stage.

RICH SWEET YEAST DOUGH

This recipe can be used for making plain or fruit buns, or for producing Continental recipes, such as the Danish Julekringle (Christmas Kringle).

For the basic dough use
180 ml (¼ pint plus 2 tablespoons) milk
25 g (1 oz) fresh yeast or 1 level tablespoon
  (½ oz) dried yeast and 1 teaspoon sugar
75 g (3 oz) butter
2 eggs
450 g (1 lb) strong or plain flour
¼ teaspoon salt
50 g (2 oz) caster sugar

BATH BUNS Add an extra 1 tablespoon milk, 1 teaspoon ground cinnamon, 175 g (6 oz) mixed dried fruit, 25–50 g (1–2 oz) chopped candied peel and 25 g (1 oz) loaf sugar for the topping.
For less soft fruit buns omit the extra tablespoon of milk. Use ordinary sugar plus 1 tablespoon boiling water to glaze after cooking.

KRINGLE Omit the extra 1 tablespoon milk under Bath Buns and the candied peel, but add 25 g (1 oz) blanched flaked almonds and an extra 25 g (1 oz) butter.

1 Heat half the milk to blood heat. If using *fresh* yeast, cream in a bowl, add the heated milk and stir to blend. If using *dried* yeast, pour the heated milk into a bowl, add the teaspoon sugar and stir to dissolve. Sprinkle on the dried yeast and stir to blend. Leave the yeast liquid in a warm place for 10–15 minutes until the mixture is frothy.
2 Heat the 75 g (3 oz) butter and remaining milk. When the butter has melted, add to the yeast mixture.

3 Whisk in the eggs.
MA 4 Sift the flour and salt into the mixer bowl (add cinnamon, fruit and peel if the recipe uses these). Add the sugar. Fix the dough hook or kneaders. Switch to the lowest speed and gradually blend in the liquid mixture from stage 3. Knead until smooth and elastic. Test if the dough is sufficiently kneaded.
FP   Place the double-bladed cutting knife and bowl in position. Sift in the flour and salt (add cinnamon if the recipe uses this). Add the sugar. Fix the lid, switch on and gradually blend in the liquid from stage 3, pouring it through the feed-tube. Knead the dough for 9–10 seconds. Test if the dough is sufficiently kneaded.

If the recipe includes dried fruit and/or candied peel, add at this stage and process for 1–2 seconds only; this makes certain the fruit is blended into the dough and **not** chopped.

5 Cover the kneaded dough with lightly oiled polythene or a clean cloth and allow to prove in a warm, but not too hot, place until doubled in size. This rich dough takes about 1¼ hours.
MA
OR 'Knock back' the dough, this means allowing the mixer or food processor to knead the dough very briefly until ready to form into shapes. Make the shapes as below; test before you begin to check that the dough has been sufficiently kneaded.
FP

BATH BUNS Make 10–12 round shapes; this softer dough spreads a great deal, so allow plenty of space on the warmed greased baking trays.

KRINGLE Form into a long 'sausage-shape'. Grease a 28 x 11-cm (11 x 7-in) tin; twist the dough to fit.

PLAIN BUNS Make 12–16 finger or round shapes. Place on warmed greased baking trays, allowing room for spreading.

6 Cover the dough with oiled polythene or a clean teacloth to prevent the outside hardening. Allow to prove until *nearly* double the original size; buns take about 20–25 minutes, the kringle from 30–40 minutes.

7 **BATH BUNS** Crush the loaf sugar into small pieces but do not make too fine. Press gently on top of the buns.

KRINGLE Melt the extra 25 g (1 oz) butter and use to brush over the dough. Crush the loaf sugar as for Bath Buns, sprinkle this and the flaked almonds on top of the dough.

8 Bake the buns just above the centre of a moderately hot to hot oven, 200–220°C, 400–425°F, Gas Mark 6–7, for about 12 minutes. Bake the kringle in the centre of a moderately hot oven, 200°C, 400°F, Gas Mark 6, for about 30 minutes.

9 If making rich fruit buns, blend the sugar and water, brush over the top of the buns as soon as they are removed from the oven.

To ice plain buns, blend 175–225 g (6–8 oz) sieved icing sugar with enough water or lemon juice to make a fairly stiff consistency. Spread over the buns when they are cold and allow to set.

To freeze
Can be frozen for 1 month.

MENUS FOR BABIES

One of the advantages of owning a blender or food processor is the ease with which meals may be prepared for a small baby, for whom all foods must be made into a smooth purée.

It is pointed out in the beginning of the book that neither the blender nor the food processor make a purée that is completely free from tough skins and very hard pips; the only electrical appliance that will do this is the sieve and colander attachment of a large mixer. Tiny babies must not be given food with skin or pips, so avoid these foods or put the purée through a hand sieve or special baby blender after using a food processor or blender. It always is surprisingly easy to sieve after blending or processing. You will however be quite satisfied with most meats, vegetables and the majority of fruits that are blended or processed.

One great advantage of preparing baby foods at home, rather than buying those sold in jars or cans, is that they fit into family meals; you are not offering a baby something different from that being eaten by the rest of the family. You are therefore educating the child to eat, and enjoy, the kind of meals he, or she, will be given at a slightly older stage.

Other obvious advantages are the saving of money – the amount of food eaten by a baby is very small, so that tiny portions of meat, fish and vegetables rarely mean extra food has to be purchased. You will also save time and effort in shopping for special baby foods. You can, and should, avoid giving the child foods that are over-sweetened, a criticism sometimes made of commercially prepared baby foods.

Kinds of foods to choose
Your doctor or clinic will make specific recommendations, but generally speaking you can include

LEAN MEAT Include beef, lamb, chicken or turkey, rabbit, liver, kidney, sweetbreads, brains and tripe, but *not* pork, veal, duck. Bacon is a good choice, but grill rather than fry.
WHITE FISH Include herrings and herring roes as the child gets a little older.
VEGETABLES If cooked by the conserved method. Avoid fried vegetables.
FRUITS Either raw or cooked as a purée. Avoid cherries, gooseberries, strawberries and dried fruits when a child is under a year old.

PRESERVES

There are many ways in which mixer attachments or a food processor can be helpful when preparing preserves.

Thinly sliced, finely chopped or puréed fruits soften within a short time, and the briefer the cooking period the better the flavour and colour of the preserve. Shredding peel, as described in the marmalade recipe, is very quickly done.

Making jams

Many jams, such as strawberry or cherry, are made with whole fruit; for it is considered that the jam looks and tastes better if it contains large pieces or even whole fruit.

There are, however, many jams, ranging from raspberry and gooseberry to cooking plums, in which the fruit is generally cooked to a pulp before adding the sugar. Save cooking time and fuel by first making a purée of the raw fruit in a blender or food processor. If the recipe recommends adding a little water to the fruit when cooking this *reduce the recommended amount* by 50 per cent, for the cooking time for the fruit will be appreciably less and therefore there will be less evaporation of liquid. Tip this purée into the preserving pan, simmer gently for a few minutes, or until the fruit is tender and hot. Stir in the sugar and continue in the usual way.

Making jelly

All fruits have to be simmered until a pulp before they are strained through a jelly bag. Speed up this process by making a purée from softer fruits in a similar way to that described under 'Making Jams' above. When preparing a jelly with hard fruit, such as cooking apples, quarter the *unpeeled* and *uncored* fruit and put these through the slicing attachment of a mixer or slicing disc of a food processor. Use the peel and cores of the apples for these provide essential pectin for setting.

The water content can be slightly reduced if the fruits for jelly are prepared in this way, i.e. use 200 ml (7½ fl oz) instead of 300 ml (½ pt).

Making chutneys

Most chutney recipes contain onions, peel and chop these as described on page 79.

Tomatoes and soft fruits can be made into a purée in a blender or food processor, and firm fruit, such as apples, peeled, cored and thinly sliced. This will speed-up the cooking time.

Do not, however, reduce the recommended amount of vinegar or sugar in a chutney, for these are essential preservatives.

ORANGE MARMALADE

1 Halve 450 g (1 lb) Seville or bitter oranges; remove the pips, and tie them in a piece of muslin.

(MA) OR (FP) 2 Extract the juice using the juice extractor attachment, or use a hand squeezer. Put on one side.

(MA) 3 Put the peel and pulp through the mincer attachment.

(FP) Chop the peel and pulp finely in the food processor using the double-bladed cutting knife.

4 Put the finely chopped oranges into a bowl with the bag of pips and cover with 1.4 litres (2½ pt) water. Soak overnight, then tip into a preserving pan.

5 Simmer gently until the peel is tender. Add 1.1 kg (2½ lb) preserving or granulated sugar and stir until dissolved. Add the orange juice and 3 tablespoons lemon juice.

6 Bring the marmalade to the boil, remove the bag of pips and boil rapidly until setting point is reached. Pot and cover as usual.

Makes about 1.9 kg (generous 4 lb)

Note This is the continental type marmalade. For ordinary marmalade, use the bean and peel slicer attachment of a large mixer and shred the peel as directed by the manufacturer.

INDEX

Page numbers in *italics* indicate illustrations